Design OF Man
J L Duncan

Design OF Man

J L Duncan

2016
Tractrix Publishing Auckland, New Zealand
tractrix n. geom. a curve of pursuit

Design of Man

ISBN: 978-0-473-37050-3

Published by Tractrix Publishing Auckland, New Zealand
tractrix n. geom. a curve of pursuit

TABLE OF CONTENTS

INTRODUCTION

Books on human behaviour are legion. It seems that authors of every conceivable background have contributed. Philosophers have tried to understand us, psychiatrists can tell us whether we are normal or otherwise, behavioural scientists have reduced us to formulae, and for a fee, will tell us how we can be manipulated.

Each tells a different story, one that derives from the writer's own training and experience. The religious writer (the inspired) will wonder,

What is man, that Thou art mindful of him?[1]

. . . and try as we might we do not find a good answer. Philosophers try a different tack, but Montaigne, the arch-pragmatist amongst them, has a warning:

Man (in good earnest) is a marvellous vain, fickle and unstable subject, and on whom it is hard to form any certain and uniform judgement.[2]

Whether the world needs another book on human behaviour is for you to decide. This one is different in that it approaches the subject from an engineering point of view and considers whether the laws of mechanics and physics that engineers use to design machines have any application to the way you and I behave.

Curiously, engineers rarely express themselves on the subject of mankind. It may be that they are more interested in their own creations. Although the world is unaware of it, engineering is a peculiarly satisfying profession. In their musings, engineers tend to turn to their own world rather than to mankind in the wider sphere. Perhaps this will change with the growth in robotics.

This book's purpose is not to equate us with machines, but to take a light-hearted examination of some of our characteristics. Strangely, the laws of mechanics do fit. This is fortunate, as these laws are fundamentally correct, unlike the so-called "laws" of other branches of learning. George Orwell pointed out that,

> **economic laws** do not operate in the same way as the law of gravity, that they can be held up for long periods by people who . . . believe in their own destiny.[3]

Newton's Laws of Motion, for example, do not need to be verified by each new generation of scientists; their field of application has some limits, but in the world that you and I inhabit, they are perfectly correct, always have been and always will be.

In other branches of learning "laws" often depend on accepted opinion and are believed if their champions are sufficiently vocal. In engineering, if a bridge does fall down, you can be quite sure that it is not because the laws of mechanics were wrong, but because the engineer applied the laws incorrectly.

Robotics, one arena in which engineers may find themselves ruminating on human nature, is about to expand on a scale that will surprise us; we are only scratching the surface at the moment, but what we have already is both exciting and perhaps alarming. It is commonplace now for the gigantic mining trucks that move overburden and ore from great holes in the ground to be driven by persons sitting in a city office a thousand miles away. Robots are extending our physical capabilities, and sooner or later we will want them to express our personality. Engineers already produce the computers that magnify our senses and our mental capabilities. The goal now is to get the computers to think, but this is not too easy. Henry Ford was well aware of the problem:

> Thinking is the hardest thing known to man,
> which is the reason it is so rarely done.[4]

Engineers will be familiar with much of what is written here. Without thinking much about it, they already apply their engineering habits when dealing with people. This book is written for those who are not engineers, in the hope that by viewing life according to a different background, they will gain some new insights.

Why do we need to look afresh at human behaviour? We, mankind, are now changing our environment on a previously unimagined scale. Traditional diplomacy and politics are clearly ineffective in controlling the problem. The solution will lie in changing our behaviour and developing new technologies. On top of this, we are also being subjected to new technologies—television, social media, instant communications, and all the devices that occupy a big part of the waking hours of people of all ages. It is just possible that looking at these new influences in the way engineers look at the conditions that affect the behaviour of machines will improve our response to the ever-changing world.

If we do this, we shall be better informed, and let us hope we shall all be a little wiser. It is time for a change. Human behaviour has been the province of the philosopher, the psychologist, and the scientist, and they are generally unaware that engineers have been developing magnificent methods of system analysis and machine control that could be applied with great effect in their studies. It is perhaps time to enlighten them.

It is said that mastering a second language not only expands your range of communication, but improves your ability with your own tongue. As Kipling said,

> . . . what should they know of England who only England know?[5]

This book looks at human behaviour through the eyes of one engineer. You have been warned that it is not a serious treatise. It is written for enjoyment, very much in the spirit of the poet who in his epitaph offered,

> Some random truths he can impart.—
>
> The harvest of a quiet eye
>
> That broods and sleeps on his own heart.[6]

I do not claim that the thoughts in this book, random or otherwise, are *truths,* but I do offer a few ideas that are simple, fun, and might even be useful.

Chapter 1
A FLAWED CREATION?

"I sometimes think that God in creating Man,
overestimated His abilities."
—Oscar Wilde

If we need a list of the questions to ask about mankind, Kipling's "serving men" are a good start:

Their names are What and Why and When

And How and Where and Who.[7]

Unfortunately, the question *why?* is just too difficult for me to tackle. Why should there be human beings, and why do they exist in such profusion? If you want to pursue this question, you will have to go elsewhere.

Engineers are used to dealing with the other demands—*what* and how. What do you need, and how will it work?

It is inevitable that in this study man should be treated as a design, but as well as avoiding the question "Why is man?" I intend to be like Falstaff,

I was a coward on instinct.[8]

and avoid discussing *who* is the designer. This is a muddy field with a quagmire in the middle and antagonists shouting as loudly as they can from one edge of the paddock to the other. Believers have it thus:

Know ye that the Lord he is God; it is he that hath made us, and not we ourselves.[9]

Those on the other side maintain that we are here purely by chance, that there is no higher power in the universe and no intelligence responsible for our existence. The experts of both persuasions do not seem to realise that humans have a strange ability to adhere to more than one idea at a time, even if the ideas contradict each other.

The credit for defining the artist as a person who can hold two inconsistent ideas at once goes to F Scott Fitzgerald. The credit for realising that that is what all modern men can do—and indeed must be able to do—belongs to Sir Walter Scott.[10]

If asked for my view on either of these stark possibilities, divine will or blind chance, my answer is, "Well, it all depends!"

As we are not going to ask that question, let us accept the obvious fact that the human race exists, by design or by chance. Though we as a species are diverse, we share so much in common that an explanation of our behaviour in the language of the engineer is worth entertaining. We can start by seeing how writers have judged us: what is the reputation of this creation, by design or by accident, that we call mankind? We must accept that all judgement is biased; all writers are human (or so we assume), and even if a writer claims to be divinely inspired, what is written is still only hearsay and filtered through the mortal mind, which we all know is an unreliable organ!

The suggestion that as human beings we are basically defective is something we would oppose, even if we have some suspicion that it might be true. There may be some bad apples in the barrel, but why cast doubt on all the good ones? As human beings, we reject the idea that we are forged in a faulty die, even if Oscar Wilde says so with wit and elegance and, if we are to believe Dorothy Parker,[11] a degree of inevitability.

> If, with the literate, I am
>
> Impelled to try an epigram,
>
> I never seek to take the credit,
>
> We all assume that Oscar said it.

It is perfectly obvious that many humans are constructed in an unfortunate way, but we like to think this is an individual failing rather than a systemic fault. Of course Wilde does not blame us for being imperfect; he neatly deflects the failing on God. This may give some solace, but not everyone believes in a Creator.

Others have managed to convey similar views about our unsatisfactory construction without introducing any gods. W S Gilbert made a fortune by showing how ridiculous we are, and he did so with cunning and without offending the clergy. He said that:

Man is Nature's sole mistake.[12]

If you are going to make a derogatory statement about your fellow man, we may infer it is best to say it in comic verse. Better yet, find a talented composer like Arthur Sullivan[13] to set it to a catchy tune. Alas, even this did not work entirely for Gilbert. He got into great trouble for making fun of that "right, regular queen," Victoria:

I don't know whether she'll wear a feather

I rather think she should.[14]

Poor Gilbert was not knighted until well after Queen Victoria died. Sullivan, who only wrote the tunes, was knighted in the prime of his life.

This idea that man is basically a faulty product is not confined to the stage. Serious philosophy also has many similar references. Friedrich Nietzche said:

Woman was God's second blunder.[15]

Robert Burns, whose delight in women would never have been understood by Nietzsche, put it in another way:

> Auld Nature swears, the lovely dears
> Her noblest work she classes, O:
> Her prentice han' she try'd on man,
> An' then she made the lasses, O.[16]

Burns is probably closer to the mark; the male is a less polished creation. Women, on the other hand, embody much that is hidden, subtle and, at least to men, wonderful but extraordinarily complicated.

Leaving aside gender differences, Arthur Koestler[17] devoted a lengthy thesis to the idea that mankind is an evolutionary event that went wrong. He argued that we all are truly one of Nature's mistakes. Koestler's book is entertaining reading, but we are not bound to accept his idea; the philosophy establishment finds him too creative and insufficiently bound by academic protocol to take seriously—or, to put it another way, Koestler's books sell, unlike the works of most philosophers.

Which "Man"?

The word *Man* with a capital M is, of course, suspect. It can mean all sorts of things, and without exactly saying so, we tend to exclude certain members of the population when we discuss *Man*.

There is *I* or *me,* for example, the right thinking, reasonable one. I may be like King John, who "had his little ways,"[18] but nevertheless I am a perfectly satisfactory creation. Those who think otherwise are wrong!

Then there is *we* or *us*—the people who think as I do even if they are not quite as reasonable as I am. They may have faults, but we will not condemn them. Thirdly, there is *them. They* are the problem. All difficulties are caused by *them.* Why do *they* exist?

The comic strip character who declared "we have met the enemy and he is us"[19] may have been guilty of bad grammar, but he has caught us out in our attempt to transfer all blame to *them.* Nevertheless, let us stick to our fiction—*we* could not possibly be wrong; it is always *them!*

I am not sure which of these three groups of Man, *I, we,* or *them,* Oscar Wilde had in mind when he chided the Creator. I suspect that before his life fell apart, he believed God had done an admirable job in creating Oscar Wilde, but sadly things changed, and after humiliation and imprisonment he wrote:

> For he that lives more lives than one,
>
> More deaths than one must die.[20]

For comfort's sake, in this discussion let "Man" be *them* and face the fact that Man is capable of some very wrong actions and does seem to be constructed inappropriately.

> Yet man is born to trouble, as surely as sparks
>
> fly upward to the sky.[21]

The Bible warns us not to look too closely at ourselves and at our existence. Doing this even on the reliable basis of engineering practice is ill-advised. Possibly we all have an inflated view of our own importance, when, in truth, we are no better than a lump of clay:

Does the clay say to the potter,

"What are you making?" . . .

Woe to him who says to his father,

"What have you begotten?"[22]

Perhaps if we take the view that,

Man is neither good nor bad; he is born with instincts and abilities.[23]

we can look at these instincts and see if, in some way, they obey the laws of physics. You may find the notion preposterous, but that is for you to decide.

As with all things, you must make up your own mind about what you believe. Samuel Butler warns of the dangers of having others form our ideas:

The public buys its opinions as it buys its meat, or takes in its milk, on the principle that it is cheaper to do so than keep a cow. So it is, but the milk is more likely to be watered.[24]

Chapter 2
THE ENGINEER

". . . 'tis the sport to have the engineer
Hoist with his own petard."
——William Shakespeare[25]

The broad plan in this book is to look at the way engineers design machines and the models they use to predict their behaviour and see if there are any analogues with human behaviour. Given that I am not writing a scientific thesis, and that, as Montaigne says, it is hard to take human behaviour seriously, the inquiry will be a meandering one.

To understand the way engineers analyse behaviour in their machines, one should first be acquainted with engineers themselves, because they are a special breed.

It is curious, but if asked to name some famous engineers, most people could think of one or two from the nineteenth century—Telford, 1757–1834, and his bridges; Stephenson, 1803–59, and his railways; or Roebling, 1806–69, and the Brooklyn Bridge. If asked for some twentieth-century names, there might be a slight hesitation. This is strange considering that the twentieth century saw the blossoming of engineering on a scale that was unprecedented.

Our general ignorance of what magnificently surrounds us and who created it does not end there. If pressed further and asked "What do engineers do?", the answer might be, "Well they sort of make things, don't they?"

Many, perhaps unconsciously, place engineers in a class similar to clean drinking water and proper sewerage—things that are important to have, but best kept out of sight. It may be that the public has been persuaded that the great advances in the modern world are due to the entrepreneur, the businessman, the corporate genius and the like, when in fact these were all carried along on a wave created by the engineer.

The lives of the Victorian engineers were written up by Samuel Smiles, 1812–1904, whose work now is more often recommended than read. In his time, Smiles was an influential writer; he was a medical doctor and also the forefather of all the writers of the "self-help" books that litter our shelves. (He was the first to popularise the motto "God helps those who help themselves"[26]). In more recent times, popular accounts of engineers and their works have not been best-sellers. One even finds a reluctance to recognise great engineers.

A particular case is that of Barnes Wallis, 1887–1979. His contributions were of national importance and covered many years. He designed the great airship, the R100, which was completely successful, unlike its competitor, the R101, which was built for political reasons and crashed ignominiously and tragically on its maiden voyage. His contributions during the Second World War, which included the "bouncing bomb" of Dam Busters' fame and the Wellington bomber, are well-known, but strangely the establishment withheld its gratitude, and he was not knighted until 1968. Perhaps the mediocrity of lesser breeds in the corridors of power had been shown up by his airship mastery, and so they obstructed his recognition.

> In a very real sense, Wallis's fame has suffered from the very fact of his being English.[27]

Although there is a general impression that engineering is a solid and worthy profession, as has been said, there is a degree of vagueness about what engineers do and how they think. A poet and writer who was intimately involved with aviation said that

> what is essential is invisible to the eye.[28]

and perhaps because engineering is essential for the working of our modern world, it is unnoticed.

The highest level of engineering is the design of machines and devices. Nothing, except the birth of one's child, is quite as rewarding as starting up a machine you have designed and built and seeing and hearing it do its work. This joy in what you have created makes the profession satisfying.

Of course, not all engineers become designers,

but they all share a knowledge of the physical world and the laws that govern it. These laws have their own truth and integrity and, as mentioned, are not subject to whim, fashion, or political expediency. The profession is thus a fulfilling one, and unlike those in so many other walks of life, engineers can generally look back on their careers and be happy and thankful for their life's work.

What are the typical characteristics of the engineer? Each profession tends to attract different kinds of people. Medicine, for example, has always attracted a few undesirables, and the profession has had to protect itself from a very early stage. For example, the Royal College of Physicians had a charter in 1518 to

> curb the audacity of those wicked men who shall profess medicine more for the sake of their avarice than from the assurance of any good conscience.

A very wise precaution!

Engineering institutions have their own charters, but protecting the profession from avarice has never been a problem. If one were to generalize about the character of engineers, it would be to say they are quietly conservative and self-effacing. The medical profession may also be conservative, but one would not use "self-effacing" to describe most of its members. Samuel Butler was so incensed by the behaviour of some medical doctors in England in the nineteenth century that he parodied the profession in his work on the mythical and nonsensical world of Erewhon[29] (located just over a mountain range in New Zealand). There, it is a criminal offence to be ill, and you should be punished. If you commit a moral wrong, that is not your fault, and you should employ a "straightener" to set you right; if you continued in your immorality, you were admitted to a kind of hospital. Butler describes a young man who is sentenced to imprisonment for having consumption, with previous convictions for aggravated bronchitis. In his summing up, the judge gives several reasons for a severe sentence, including the need to deter "a class of men who lie hidden among us, and who are called physicians."

The judge warns that without severe measures

taken against the criminally ill, physicians would flourish.

> The head of the household would become subordinate to the family doctor, who would interfere between man and wife, between master and servant, until doctors should be the only depositaries of power in the nation, and have all that we hold precious at their mercy. A time of universal dephysicalization would ensue; medicine-vendors of all kinds would abound in our streets and advertise in all our newspapers.[30]

One wonders whether the world of Erewhon is still mythical. We are overwhelmed both with "medicine-vendors" and sociologists who convince the courts that people are not responsible for their morally reprehensible acts. Unfortunately, neither the physician nor the psychiatrist is making progress in useful directions; we still have endemic ailments, including the common cold and moral turpitude!

If you wish to become more informed about engineers, you will find that the literature is meagre. A good autobiography is *Slide Rule* by Nevil Shute.[31] Early in his career he assisted Barnes Wallis in the design of the R100 airship, and his description of its maiden voyage from England to Canada and back is magnificent. Shute formed his own successful aircraft company and for the latter part of the Second World War served in the Royal Navy. (To juniors like me, he was always addressed with great respect as "Commander Norway.") Many of Shute's novels are about engineers, and while his literary talents are not highly regarded, his books will probably survive better than those of some of our contemporary literary lions (and lionesses).

Another writer who had a deep understanding of and great appreciation for engineering was Rudyard Kipling. Like Shute his talents are often looked down upon, but as George Orwell said,

> During five literary generations every enlightened person has despised him, and at the end of that time nine-tenths of these enlightened persons are forgotten and Kipling is in some sense still there.[32]

In 1907, Kipling was asked to write a poem to commemorate engineering in Canada. In a brilliant and fitting way he alluded to the biblical story of Mary and Martha, the sisters who entertained Jesus in their house. Martha was busy making sure that all were fed and looked after while Mary sat at the feet of Jesus.

> But Martha was distracted by all the preparations that had to be made. She came to him and asked, "Lord, don't you care that my sister has left me to do all the work by myself? Tell her to help me!"

> "Martha, Martha," the Lord answered, "you are worried and upset about many things, but only one thing is needed. Mary has chosen what is better, and it will not be taken away from her."[33]

Kipling's view was that engineers are epitomised by Martha:

> The Sons of Mary seldom bother, for they have inherited that good part;

> But the Sons of Martha favour their Mother

of the careful soul and the troubled heart.

And because she lost her temper once, and because she was rude to the Lord her Guest,

Her Sons must wait upon Mary's Sons, world without end, reprieve, or rest.

It is their care in all the ages to take the buffet and cushion the shock.

It is their care that the gear engages; it is their care that the switches lock.

It is their care that the wheels run truly; it is their care to embark and entrain,

Tally, transport, and deliver duly the Sons of Mary by land and main

. . .

And the Sons of Mary smile and are blessèd— they know the Angels are on their side.

They know in them is the Grace confessèd, and for them are the Mercies multiplied.

They sit at the feet—they hear the Word— they see how truly the Promise runs.

They have cast their burden upon the Lord, and—the Lord He lays it on Martha's Sons![34]

To this day, Canadian engineers upon graduation are invited to become "Sons and Daughters of Martha" and asked to wear an iron ring as a symbol of their special place. The ring is made of steel salvaged from an engineering disaster, and it reminds them of the danger to life, limb, and property should they do their job improperly.

As well as thinking about what engineers are like, in order to tackle our subject fully we need to think about what they do. In a rare philosophical moment, President Mahid[35] of Indonesia deplored the practice of sending only scientists and technologists overseas for education and not including scholars of the liberal arts. He said of engineers:

> Analysing problems in a reductionist fashion and rigorously applying simple formulas may be an appropriate approach to building a bridge, or even erecting a skyscraper, but it is grossly inappropriate and inadequate to the task of building modern Muslim society.[36]

One can agree with President Mahid that if a country wishes to send young people overseas to learn from other nations, it should not send only scientists and technologists. It should also send those who excel in the liberal arts. The benefit derived from young people having experiences outside their own country is quite evident. A good example is seen in China. Deng Xiaoping (1904–97) lived in France and Zhou Enlai (1898–1976) in Japan when they were young. They returned to their own country, and later in life, when they became influential, they led China out of the abyss of the Cultural Revolution. Mahid was right in part of his statement, but he was mistaken in his understanding of what engineers do.

It is true that bridges, skyscrapers, and even large ships can be designed by "applying simple formulas"—although in fairness to the technologists who do this, the formulas are not simple. This method is called "rule book design," and it works provided that construction follows accepted practice, that materials conform to familiar grades, and that the scope of the project remains within existing limits. It is similar to the way pre-engineering guilds of artisans worked. They were not sure why some cathedrals fell down and others did not, so they developed rules to be followed based on the examples that worked.

Modern rule book design is carried out by technologists, but the rules themselves are created and systematized by engineers. The calculations are done by technologists, but the overall project must be supervised by engineers to ensure that the work remains within the limits of the rule book.

Unfortunately, some companies have taken the view that because they can do without engineers (at least in the short term), they can save money by only employing technologists. This has led to disaster.

An example is found in steel bridges. About fifty years ago, higher strength steels were introduced. Because the rules for testing and welding were not revised adequately, problems, including total collapse, occurred. Also, because of the higher strength, thinner steel could be used. The steel was strong enough so that parts of the bridge were not pulled apart, but all bridges have areas that are subject to compressive forces. These regions may fail by buckling or crumpling up, and the likelihood of this depends more on thickness than on strength. Several accidents have occurred due to buckling and total collapse, and lives were lost, including, in Australia, that of one of my fellow students.

J E Gordon, 1913–98, was intimately involved in the development of strong materials, and his book *The New Science of Strong Materials* contains important insights (as well as some penetrating quips about the personalities of engineers). He himself was a designer, and he remarked that he often worried about some particular aspect of a design, but strangely enough, the disasters he worried about never happened. There is an important lesson here: a designer should always be a worrier!

Thomas Telford, described as "the greatest civil engineer of his generation,"[36] designed and supervised the construction of the Menai Straits suspension bridge. When it was opened in 1826, it was the largest suspension bridge ever built. The story goes that everyone gathered to see if his bridge would hold up. When it did, the local dignitaries were busy congratulating themselves on having managed a successful enterprise, but the builder was not amongst them. Eventually he was found, standing away from the bustle, quietly thanking his Maker for guidance and a safe outcome. *He knew what could go wrong.* That is the hallmark of a good designer.

It is significant that engineering is the only profession that has developed the concept of the factor of safety to such a high level and applied it rigorously in all designs. Other professions have yet to embrace the concept fully. The dismal performance of much-vaunted "due diligence" in the financial and corporate communities shows how far behind they are.

The conservatism, care, and responsibility of engineers are largely voluntary and self-imposed. It is true that there are manifold laws and rules governing safety in their profession, but as we know, these require a genuine desire on the part of the ruled to act safely if they are to be successful.

The modern aircraft engine is extraordinarily safe. Following Saint Expury's rule, the engines are invisible and neatly concealed within smooth nacelles. If the nacelles are removed and the engine exposed, it is seen to be an amazingly complex collection of pumps, piping, control devices, and instrumentation. It reminds one of the abdomen of an animal when the skin has been removed by the butcher and a mass of organs—heart, lungs, kidneys, and many others—are exposed. All are essential for maintaining life, and they are packed neatly and invisibly in the body. Similarly, every component in an aircraft engine is vital and necessary, and the whole is complicated. To the passenger, the critical components are totally out of sight.

The fact that these engines can take a plane many times around the world with a minimum of maintenance is due to the skill, care, and integrity of the engineers who design, build, and maintain aircraft. The record is amazingly good. Each day there are tens of thousands of commercial flights, and accidents are very few indeed. Governments and regulators should remember that this situation requires constant attention. If money is diverted from proper engineering procedures, if engineers fail to maintain their standards and lose their influence, aircraft will fall out of the sky with the same frequency that corporations and financial institutes now fail.

The engineer, then, is by nature conservative, cautious, a bit of a worrier, always looking for what might go wrong, acknowledging the uncertainty of his analyses and factoring in the appropriate allowances. If you think this makes engineers dull company, this may be your problem; engineers, on the whole, enjoy the company of their colleagues. At the present time, when the effect of industrial activity on world climate is becoming crucial, the need for reliable analysis and effective ways of dealing with climate change is creating a challenge of greater magnitude than we have ever seen before. The engineers will continue to be the sons and daughters of Martha and try to limit the damage, but it may be a losing battle. Everyone must face the challenge. As the medieval Saint Teresa of Avila[37] said:

> To give the Lord a perfect hospitality, Mary
> and Martha must combine.

This was a courageous statement, as the hierarchy of the church at the time were men who had gained their power by sitting at the feet of the mighty rather than by putting food on the table. In our day, when financiers, businessmen, and politicians are motivated mainly by self-interest and have their feet firmly in the trough of private and public funding, the outlook is not good.

In his own time, Telford changed the face of his country more than anyone. Perhaps foreseeing how things would evolve, he said:

> I hold that the aim and end of all ought not
> to be a mere bag of money, but something far
> higher and better.[38]

So much of what we see suggests that the financial world is only concerned with the "bag of money." Only if the Marys and the Marthas of this world can learn to cooperate and act with integrity will mankind avoid the hiding it richly deserves!

Chapter 3
DESIGN AND DEVELOPMENT

"Nature does not proceed by leaps."
—Carolus Linnaeus[39]

Evolution is a slow process, but the same cannot be said of engineering and science. In engineering, the rate of change during the last century was enormous. In 1900 there were few cars on the road and no houses with electricity; by 2000, there were too many cars and we were totally dependent on electricity.

The nineteenth and twentieth centuries saw the greatest revolution of all time, different in kind from the French or American revolutions and much greater in its effect. It was a revolution of things—engines, motor cars, pharmaceuticals, computers, aeroplanes, communications. We have not yet had the historians nor the philosophers to explain it to us, and we do not understand it. We do not know yet if the revolution is over, or who or what won.

> O God! That one might read the book of fate,
>
> And see the revolution of the times.[40]

This is a key thought. We live in a revolution that we do not understand. Things have changed so much. Life today is vastly different from life fifty years ago, and the pace of change continues to accelerate. The differences have been brought about largely by engineering and technology.

Starting in the eighteenth century, clever people began to design machines and devices of a kind that did not previously exist, beginning with steam engines that pumped water out of mines and progressing in the nineteenth century to locomotives and giant turbines to generate electricity. Aircraft came about not because of some discovery in aerodynamics, but because the Wright brothers and others designed and built aircraft in which propulsion, controls, and structure were all combined in a product that worked. The same is true with motor cars, the chemical industry, and all other parts of industry today. Individual steps in the process have all occurred because of design.

My quest is to see if the processes that delivered these enormous changes can be applied in some way to understanding human behaviour. This inevitably requires a step-by-step analysis. In the previous chapter, I described engineers and their profession. In this chapter, my objective is to explain the concept of *engineering design.*

Most people would say they understand what is meant by the word design, but in engineering it has a particular meaning, and there are strict rules that apply. Some time ago, the engineering school of which I was part sought to attract a lively designer. He told us he had designed the latest snowmobile. (As the school was in Canada, this had much more impact than it would have had in a more temperate climate!) I visited the company where he worked in order to see his design. What I found was that the latest snowmobile was very good, but it was not basically different from the previous model. What he had done was to select the colours, the stripes, and the paint job, and he had done this well. To him, he had "designed" the machine. To a hoary and conservative engineer like me, this was *styling*, not *design!*

Fortunately, we did attract him, and he became a valued member of our team, teaching design (not styling).

There are many kinds of design, from fashion design to product design in a finance company. They all have their place. What I intend here is to describe briefly the strict nature of engineering design and the rules that apply.

The scientific method is often discussed in schools, but little is heard of the process of engineering design, even though it has clear rules and a well-established formalism. Engineers do not have a monopoly on designing new things, but there are special rules for *engineering design* that distinguish it from innovation in general. During the last 150 years, engineers have established rules and a code of practice governing their work. This ensures a level of certainty not delivered by other professions. Mistakes can still be made, as Rudyard Kipling pointed out many years ago:

> The careful text-books measure
> (Let all who build beware!)
> The load, the shock, the pressure
> Material can bear.
> So, when the buckled girder
> Lets down the grinding span,
> The blame of loss, or murder,
> Is laid upon the man.
> Not on the Stuff—the Man![41]

The laws of physics and the codes of engineering are not wrong and never will be. Disasters come when men or women ignore them or misinterpret them. It is an interesting aside that Kipling seems to have considered engineering as entirely a male activity, and yet his wife came from an extraordinarily artistic and creative family. In the above poem, to him "man" meant men, while today our world is not compartmentalised by gender, and certainly not so in engineering.

The key part of engineering design is that there is a guarantee that the product, if built strictly to instructions, will work and meet a specified performance. Engineers may well design something as a trial to see how and if it will work, but that is a different activity. An engineering design is not complete until it has a comprehensive proof of performance. There is a penalty in providing this assurance—the design cost is extended; the product may perform better than needed; it may be heavier and more costly than one that is proved not by prior calculation and analysis before being built, but by testing after construction. For these reasons, alternative methods may be used.

Introducing students into the design process is a delight. They have spent many hours acquiring knowledge and learning analytical techniques, and suddenly they are faced with a problem that may have many answers. A design exercise starts with a brief—a statement of what the product will do. It does not say *how* it will do this. Students know that design is a creative exercise and immediately start thinking of possible ways to meet the desired function. The trick is to let them find out for themselves that they are starting at the wrong point.

A classroom technique that works well is to hand out the brief to each student and then say nothing. Tutors move around the class, but they are carefully rehearsed in the technique of not answering any questions. Instead, they help a student by immediately asking a question in return. A likely question from a student is "What, exactly, do you want me to do?" The response is: "Have you read the brief carefully?"

The process continues, and then a student will ask, "Do you think such and such a device would work?" The response: "Have you shown it will do the job?"

Tutors know they are getting somewhere when a student's eyes suddenly light up and he says, "You are not going to tell me, are you?" At this point the tutor can break the rules and give the answer, which is: "No!"

The reason for this subterfuge is that the proper procedure for design is counterintuitive. You must suppress all thoughts about the device you will choose and *how* it will work until you have completely analysed *what* it must do—the function.

If you are asked to design a bridge to cross a certain waterway, you can start by thinking about whether it should be a girder bridge, a suspension span, an arch, or whatever, but it is a waste of time to think such thoughts. You must analyse the function first. What is the shape of the banks on either side? Where is the bed of the waterway, and what is it composed of? Given the traffic, how wide will it be, and what weight will it carry? You must establish completely the space or the box into which your design must fit, and only then can you go on to the next step, which is the selection of the mechanism or type of device that will fit the requirements—the *how* it will work. You must deliberately suppress the innovative thoughts about *how* your design will work until you have fully established *what* it must do.

Often, if you have analysed the function well, the best selection becomes self-evident. That can be a bit disappointing. Design is a creative exercise, but it is one in which the imagination must work under severe constraints of space, available materials, and the laws of nature.

Engineering design is not a monolithic method. Many variations exist, but they all share the one common factor. The artist may be like Longfellow:

> I shot an arrow in the air, it came to earth I know not where.[42]

but the engineer has a definite aim:

> If you would hit the mark, you must aim a little above it.[43]

The stakes are always high. If the steam turbine that provides your power blows up, it will destroy the building that houses it, and generally there is loss of life. Similarly, a major bridge *must* stand up.

Although components and materials can be tested individually, the whole design must be shown on paper to work before construction starts. The design is proved by analysis and careful comparison with existing practice. Since a margin of uncertainty exists in any calculation, each component must be designed for a greater load than we know it will bear—the aforementioned "safety factor" is applied.

This safety factor may be two or three or sometimes more. That is to say that the calculation must show that the component can sustain a load two or three time greater than is actually required. The consequence is that while all elements in a design are adequate, most, if not all, will be excessive. Some will be only a little better than need be, while others may be much more robust than is required. In total, the product is not as efficient as it might be, and it will be more costly than one in which each part is just adequate. A chain is only as strong as its weakest link; the problem in design is that we can never be certain which is the weakest link, so they all must be designed to be stronger than need be.

You may think that engineering design is a wasteful process. To some degree it is, but one only has to look at other professions to see the consequences of not demanding this level of safety. Throughout the world, immense high-rise office buildings have been built to house businesses. From an engineering viewpoint, the required performance of the building is that it should not fall down. The system of design must be working: such an event, in fact, is virtually unknown. This is in sharp contrast to the performance of the companies that inhabit these buildings. If the structural failure rate of the buildings was similar to the financial failure rate of the businesses that inhabit them, every major city in the world would resemble a bomb site!

There is, however, an engineering alternative to design, and this is the process of development. One or more prototypes are designed and built. They do not have to meet the required performance the first time. They are first tested, and the parts that are shown to be weak links are modified. The first method, *engineering design,* consists of working backwards from the specified task and proving by calculation, analysis, or comparison with existing practice that the device will work without modification. The alternative, *development,* consists of making one's best shot without having to guarantee that everything will work. The prototype is then refined by repeated testing and redesign and eliminating the weak links. Clearly, development will result in a more efficient product, but how long it will take and how much it will cost to reach the desired goal is uncertain.

There are, of course, intermediate approaches. When they create a new airliner, designers must ensure that the first one built will actually fly, but they do leave space for some testing and development to reach the desired level of performance. That said, there is enormous pressure to ensure that the prototype is very nearly the same as the final product, because the time required to create the assembly line is so great that it must be built almost simultaneously with the prototype. One does not want to have to change both the aircraft and the assembly line!

A FAMOUS ILLUSTRATION

An historic meeting between two famous British engineers illustrates the contrast between "engineering design" and "development." This event and its historic significance are described well in the books of RR Whyte.[44] In 1938, the British government established a programme to build a jet engine. Two farsighted engineers, DAA Griffith of the Royal Aircraft Establishment and Sir Frank Whittle, had established the concept and the principle, but what was needed was an actual engine.

A major component of such an engine is a turbine. A jet engine must have a turbine linked to a compressor to bring the air to a high pressure before burning the fuel. The reason for this is not obvious, but the general thermodynamic principle was understood by a French military engineer, Carnot,[45] two hundred years previously. In 1887, Parsons[46] had demonstrated the practicality of the steam turbine when he used one to power a small ship, the *Turbinia*. This ship totally embarrassed the British navy by charging through the established fleet, while it was being reviewed by Queen Victoria. The *Turbinia* went so fast that the navy, with its old-fashioned engines, could not catch it and drive it away from the royal performance!

By 1938, the company Metropolitan Vickers knew all about steam turbines and nothing about aircraft engines. Rolls-Royce, on the other hand, was the premiere builder of aircraft engines of the conventional type but had no knowledge of turbines. The government, with unusual wisdom, forced them to meet in the hope that by working together they could design and build the new kind of compressor and turbine needed for an aircraft engine.

The initial meeting is described by RR Whyte, who, as a young engineer, was assigned to the small team that built the first jet engine. The Rolls-Royce chairman, who later became Lord Hives, visited Metropolitan Vickers in Manchester and was shown around by the senior turbine engineer, Dr Karl Baumann. Large turbines in various stages of construction were on display, each destined for a large power station. Hives must have felt that he had strayed into a totally unfamiliar world, and he asked, "Where are the prototypes?" With any new engine, he told them, Rolls-Royce made six prototypes and ran them to destruction to determine the weak points. This was hardly feasible with a large steam turbine—testing large steam turbines to destruction is not an option! Failure of a large turbine resembles the explosion of a very big bomb, with similar loss of life. Hives had to be told that "there are no prototypes"! Metropolitan Vickers had to get their turbines right the first time. On the other hand, Rolls-Royce knew that if they built an engine that would not fail the first time it was run, it would be too heavy to get off the ground.

Because the sizes of their products and the tasks they performed were so different, the companies had diametrically opposite design philosophies. Rolls-Royce engineers designed the prototype as best they could, but it did not have to reach the desired performance the first time. Failure was a contained event. Rolls-Royce engineers relied heavily on the process of development to refine the design and obtain the maximum power for the minimum weight. Their refinements were beyond the scope of calculation and were justified by experiment. Metropolitan Vickers, on the other hand, could only test their product when it had been installed in the power station and connected to the boilers, and even then they could not risk a catastrophic failure. By the time they could test their product, it was too late to make major changes. They had to rely on calculation and careful comparison with previous performance to prove in the design phase that what they built would work the first time.

Both companies were quite correct in their approach, but they were operating at opposite ends of the design spectrum. "Engineering design" and "development" are both acceptable methods in engineering. The choice depends on scale, resources, and the degree of refinement required.

A FOOTNOTE

Support of jet engine development by the British government might not have happened had it not been for a lucky accident. Sir Frank Whittle had written to Prime Minister Churchill urging work on the jet engine; the letter was dealt with by his private secretary, who, no doubt, had been beautifully educated in the classics or history or both but had no idea about engineering. In his words:

> I therefore paused over the letter from an inventor who said he had discovered a way of making aeroplanes travel by blowing gases out behind instead of the, to me, obviously essential device of propeller in the front. The letter was signed "F Whittle (Group Captain)" and although clearly only a crank could have such absurd ideas, his style differed notably from that of most lunatics . . .[47]

The letter and the project might well have

passed into oblivion had not the right person happened to walk into the room at that moment. Lord Brabazon, the Minister of Aircraft Production, fortunately did know what to do with Whittle's letter—and the rest is history.

People now are quite comfortable with planes that fly without propellers, but the level of indifference about it all is so high that probably not one person in fifty or even one hundred could give you a reasonable explanation of how a jet engine drives the plane. "It just does," we would be told. And yet without these engines, the cost of international air travel would be so high that most of us would still be traveling by ship. It is recounted that

> . . . some years after the war Whittle bought a ticket to fly to America on a Pan American aircraft. He was met at the airport by an official who returned the cost of his ticket and told him that whenever he chose to fly with them, he would be welcome to do so free of charge since, but for him, they would not have the magnificent aeroplanes in which they could now invite him to be a passenger at their expense.[48]

Not only does this show the characteristic generosity of Americans in those times but also that, like the prophet, the British engineer

> is not without honour, save in his own country, and in his own house. [49]

DESIGN OPTIONS

The end point of a design is a set of instructions that completely defines what is to be built. One still occasionally hears the term *blueprint,* although most people have never seen one of these. (They were made by an early method of reproducing black-and-white drawings that resulted in white lines on a blue background.)

At one extreme, the design is proved completely by analysis and calculation and the product is guaranteed to work if built as instructed. At another level, a prototype is built and the product developed by testing to find the weak points and modifying them. At yet another level, if the product is very similar to one that exists, the design may be created from a rule book, as described in a previous chapter. With the power of modern computers, there is a further option. A virtual product can be created in the computer and "tested" and modified by more computer programs. The power of this approach is enormous, as the design codes for a ship or a skyscraper can be set up within the computer and the "performance" of the product checked in great detail.

It is interesting to compare the method of computation now with that described by Nevil Shute only eighty years ago. He was in charge of the computers that checked the structural integrity of each strut and girder in the R100 airship. The computers were not as we picture them today, but were real people, many of them in a large office carrying out calculations—often using a slide rule!

We live now in a wonderful world where all the calculations performed by a roomful of people over the course of a week can now be performed in the twinkling of an eye by a computer. In this new world it is good to remember the saying of my professor of structural engineering:

> The strength of a bolted joint depends on the bolts in it and not on the method of analysis!

In other words, do not lose touch with the real thing.

The pre-eminence of Britain in the nineteenth century came about from the quality and success of its designs in shipping, railways, steelmaking, textiles, mining, pottery, and many other fields. The US automobile industry developed in the twentieth century from the design skills of Henry Ford[50] and Walter Chrysler,[51] amongst many others. Governments have realised the link between design and economic, industrial, and to some extent social development and have set up bodies such as the British National Advisory Board on Creative and Cultural Education. Other nations have departments or ministries with titles that incorporate the words *innovation* and *industrial design.* One wishes them well, but the very names conjure up a faint Orwellian whiff! We want to have more innovation in what we do, but often the mechanism for achieving this eludes us.

Chapter 4
NATURAL FREQUENCY

"I got rhythm, I got music,
. . . Who could ask for anything more?"
—Ira Gershwin, "I Got Rhythm" (1930)

Modern engineering could be said to start with Galileo[52] and his pendulum. The legend is that while sitting in the cathedral, Galileo noticed that chandeliers that were hung on chains of equal length were swinging in the wind at the same rate. Chandeliers hung from chains of different lengths were swinging at different speeds. He thought deeply about this and came to understand a lot about the pendulum, but more importantly, he was the first man to think about force and gravity in a modern way.

(One must issue a warning about contemplating such things in church instead of listening to the sermon. Galileo had no end of trouble with the authorities, and the validity of his scientific work was not recognised by the Vatican until 1993.[53] That he had to wait 350 years to be accepted says, perhaps, more about organised religion than about Galileo.)

Galileo realised that the period, i.e. the time to complete one whole swing backward and forward, depends on the length of the pendulum and not the mass of the weight or bob. This is surprising, as we would think that a more massive body would move more slowly. But we can find the reason with a little thought. A pendulum consists of a light rod with a pivot at the top and a weight at the bottom. If the pendulum is stationary, the force in the rod exactly balances the weight force of the bob. If we use our finger to move the bob off-centre, the force we must exert depends on the weight (mass and gravity) and the angle the rod makes with the vertical. If the length of the rod is short, the angle is great and so is the force. If we hold the pendulum still, the weight force, the rod force, and our finger force are all in equilibrium. If we let go, the forces are no longer in equilibrium, and a restoring force accelerates the pendulum toward its rest position.

Some years later, Newton stated the law relating mass and acceleration, but one suspects that Galileo had some understanding of this. Newton's law is that the acceleration of a massive body is proportional to the force acting on it and inversely proportional to the mass of the body. With the pendulum, we have seen that the force that accelerates the bob back to its mid-position is proportional to the length of the rod and the weight force due to mass and gravity, while the acceleration is inversely proportional to the mass. Therefore the effect of mass cancels out. The motion of the pendulum depends only on the length of the rod and on gravity.

It took a great amount of thinking originally to work this out, and in doing so, giants like Galileo and Newton came to understand concepts such as force and motion in a way that enabled engineering to develop on a firm foundation that the artisans of former eras had lacked. This is a good example of how engineering builds on science even though the science is incomplete. The noted physicist,

Richard Feynman, 1918–88, pointed out that although we know the relation between force, mass, and acceleration, we do not know *why* mass has this property of resisting acceleration. Engineers can still make use of scientific knowledge even if it is incomplete.

This analysis of the pendulum is now learned by students at school and might occupy half an hour of class time. They would learn that the period, *T,* of a pendulum for small swings is

$$T = 2\pi\sqrt{(L/g)}$$

where *L* is the length of the rod and *g* is the local acceleration due to gravity.

(This is a nice equation; the symbol *pi* gives it a hint of universality, and the square root makes it look important. Mathematicians always feel more important when they have something in their equations that is nonlinear!)

One fears that many students, if asked why the period of a pendulum is not affected by the mass of the bob, would reply that it is *because mass does not appear in the equation.* A person with such a mind might possibly become a clockmaker but would never invent anything.

Confucius had a similar fear. Two-and-a-half thousand years ago he said:

> He who learns but does not think is lost. He who thinks but does not learn is in great danger.[54]

The important thing is not remembering the formula, but understanding why it has this particular form.

If we want the pendulum to keep swinging, we must add a small amount of energy to overcome friction losses. In a clock, this is done by a lever that engages in a slot in the rod and is connected to the escape mechanism. At just the right moment, as the bob approaches its central position, the lever exerts a small impulse. In clocks with a short rod and in which the pendulum wags back and forth excessively, the impulse needed is large and frequent. These clocks must be wound often and do not keep good time. (Some people are like this. They wag back and forth at a great rate, need to be wound up often, and are not good timekeepers.)

In the Victorian era, the Viennese regulator was a popular style of clock. Its pendulum rod was nearly a metre long, and the amplitude of the swing was so small that one had to look closely to see that it was still going. These clocks only had to be wound infrequently and were excellent time-keepers. Nowadays clocks are so reliable and accurate that we tend not to notice them, but in times gone by they were good friends.

There is a story of an old man whose living room was full of clocks. The priest was visiting, and finding that chiming the hour took at least twenty minutes, he asked the old man why he had so many clocks when they all told a different time. The answer was, "Well, Father, if they all told the same time, what would be the point of having so many?" Perhaps this is why we have so many friends. If the performance and personality of each was identical, we would only need one.

RESPONSE TIME

Just before the Second World War, RR Whyte, a mentor and friend of mine and already introduced in chapter 3, was a junior engineer in the turbine division of Metropolitan Vickers. His job was to watch over the machining of the giant steel ingots as they were transformed into massive turbine shafts.

It was obviously a highly skilled and critical job, and being young and keen to advance in the world, Whyte discovered ways to improve the process. Unfortunately, he could not convince his boss to take up any of his ideas. His work was organised in such a way that he would have a weekly meeting with his manager to run over progress with the orders in the machine shop. During these meetings he would try to interest his boss in one of his new ideas, but each time he was unsuccessful. It became very frustrating.

Fortunately, Whyte had a friend in a related area of the works, and he discussed the problem with him. The friend was not at all surprised at the manager's behaviour. He immediately asked, "Well, have you worked out his response time?"

Whyte's reply was the same as you and I would probably make. "No. What's that?"

The friend explained that each one of us, when

faced with a new idea, will immediately have a negative reaction. This gives us time to figure out what we should think and do. After a while, the negative state changes to a positive one—it may not be acceptance, but at least it is not rejection, and we start to consider the advantages or disadvantages.

The peculiar thing is that this time interval, which in engineering we would call the response time but in humans we could perhaps call the "incubation period," is different for each person—yours is different from mine—but for each of us the period is a constant. It is something we are born with, and though it varies widely throughout the population, for any individual it does not change; it is an individual characteristic like the colour of your eyes or the length of your nose.

His friend advised him, "I know your boss and have studied him. I am convinced that his response time is about one week. What you have to do is go through your weekly meeting and stick closely to your report on work in progress. Do not try to interest him in any new idea, but as you are gathering up your papers and are halfway to the door, just say, 'I am sure the productivity of

No. 2 Lathe can be improved, but I don't think my idea is much good, so I won't trouble you with it.' It is highly likely that at next week's meeting your manager will say to you, 'Whyte, I have some ideas about improving the productivity of No.2 Lathe and can probably give you a few leads, but you might just take a look at it, and next week we can discuss this." Thus his idea would eventually be accepted, even though he would not receive the credit. Perhaps his boss might say, "Young Whyte is very good provided you give him the ideas, but he is not innovative himself!" When we are making our careers, it is necessary sometimes to be satisfied with half a bone!

Whyte learnt this lesson well. He went on to become a most successful and highly respected engineer. His involvement in the first jet engine, described in chapter 3, meant that he understood how innovation worked in industry, and he would have had no difficulty in understanding that, like the pendulum, we all swing at our own characteristic frequency.

To Whyte, human behaviour was often a conundrum, but if there was a mechanical analogue of some aspect of behaviour—such as the response to a new idea and the swinging of a pendulum—then he could plan his campaigns for innovation or acceptance on an engineering basis. He would see that if we want a person to be sympathetic to our ideas and "swing along with us," we must first make the suggestion and move them slightly out of their comfort zone. We then let them swing in their own time and only give them a push at just the right moment. The thing we must not do is try to make them swing at anything other than their own natural frequency.

Behavioural scientists will know all about this and will have their own vocabulary to describe it—unfortunately, it will not make much sense to some of us, and we are happier with mechanical models that we do understand.

It is probably not a good idea to let your friends or colleagues know that you are thinking of them as though they were a pendulum, but we all swing backward and forward, and the comparison has been made before. Over one hundred years ago, an American writer said:

Old age brings along with its uglinesses the comfort that you will soon be out of it,—which ought to be a substantial relief to such discontented pendulums as we are. To be out of the war, out of debt, out of the drouth, out of the blues, out of the dentist's hands, out of the second thoughts, mortifications, and remorses that inflict such twinges and shooting pains,—out of the next winter, and the high prices, and company below your ambition—surely these are soothing hints.[55]

Poor Emerson must have been having a bad day when he wrote this, and he was not out of it as quickly as he might have hoped; he lived on for a further twenty years. Old age has its bad moments, and we are all pendulums, discontented or otherwise, but let us not give age too bad a name. It is another season in life which, on balance, is as good as any other.

To every thing there is a season, and a time to every purpose under the heaven:

> A time to be born, and a time to die; a time to plant, and a time to pluck up that which is planted.[56]

The natural frequency of a freely swinging body is one of the simplest phenomena in the general field of vibrations. The study of mechanics includes other phenomena which resemble the way people behave; they, too, are worth thinking about.

Chapter 5
RESONANCE

"Only when you are empty are you at a standstill."
—Khalil Gibran, *The Prophet*

We all swing back and forth like the pendulum. Sometimes our motion is hardly detectable, at other times it can be strong. In extreme cases, our swings may become so violent we come off our bearings and crash to the ground. What causes this? Is it the big adversities that set us off? For the most part we can endure the

Slings and arrows of outrageous fortune. [57]

Perhaps it is the little things of life, things we

do not notice that influence our moods? Is there an analogue in the world of mechanics? There certainly is. It is a phenomenon in engineering that sometimes is a curse and at other times a valuable tool. Its name is resonance.

Like our own mood swings, the swing of a pendulum is a vibration, albeit a slow one, and vibrations arise because energy is moved from one state to another with very little resistance. At the bottom of the swing, when the pendulum is moving at its fastest, the energy is entirely that of motion—*kinetic energy,* to use the proper name. At the extreme position, when the pendulum is stationary, the energy is that of a weight raised above its lowest position, the so-called *potential energy* which is proportional to mass, gravity and the distance of the weight above the bottom position.

Engineers have their own short-hand for these energies. Potential energy is $PE=mgh,$ where mg is the force to move against gravity and h is the vertical distance moved. Kinetic energy is $KE=1/2\,mV^2$. Engineers are instinctively sensitive to the power of a variable in any equation. Kinetic energy is proportional to the velocity, $V,$ raised to the power, *2,*

(V multiplied by V), indicating that the energy increases very rapidly as the speed increases. In some instances, a quantity is related to a variable raised to the power of *3,* and there are rare cases where a power of *4* or, *5,* appears. The message when the power is greater than *1* is always "beware."

People in general do not carry these equations around in their heads, although they would be better off if they did. Surprisingly, many will remember Einstein's equation relating energy to mass and the speed of light, $E=mc^2$, although only one person in a million (the person designing a nuclear power station) will have any use for it; but few will remember the kinetic energy equation even though it affects us daily. If you accelerate your car from 60 kilometres per hour to 80, the kinetic energy increases in the proportion of 36 to 64; it almost doubles. If you increase to 100 kmph, it nearly triples. If you are unfortunate enough to hit anything solid at these speeds, the kinetic energy must be dissipated in bent metal and broken bones. The traffic engineer and car designer know this well and only wish that the general public would show the respect that speed deserves. They must feel like the prophet, Isaiah, who told his people to slow down.

> In returning and rest shall ye be saved, . . .
>
> But ye said, No.[58]

Experts in other fields can perhaps tell you the energy states we move between in our mood swings. Nietzsche seems to suggest that at one extreme is the energy or exhilaration we feel when we believe we are moving toward salvation (although your idea of salvation could be different from mine), and at the other extreme is anxiety when we fear that all is falling apart. We may never know the complete story, but if we can understand how vibrations arise in mechanics and the laws governing their control, we might be able to understand more happily our own ups and downs.

THE CRYSTAL SET

One hundred or more years ago, the crystal set played a key role in the development of modern electronics. People were beginning to transmit radio signals, and many boys built their own radio—

a crystal set—to receive these signals. Pocket money was sufficient for the few bits needed, and the rest was made from cardboard, wood, and some wire. The reception was weak and could only be heard with headphones, but the remarkable thing was that it needed no batteries and yet could pick up the distant, low-powered transmissions of those days. The programmes were also rudimentary, but the joy of listening on a device you had made yourself was immense.

This may seem incredible in today's world where we are bombarded to the point of saturation with broadcasts of all kinds. Nevertheless, this is what excited people then.

My mother, who was born more than a century ago, told me that as a young girl she was furious when her older brother, who had taken her to a dance, told her just as things were warming up that they had to go home so that he could hear the twelve o'clock time signal on his crystal set!

Nowadays, so many are umbilically connected to their mobile phones or other devices that they are unaware of the marvel of it; if anything, they are bored rather than excited. Perhaps the difference with the crystal set was the personal connection; *you* had built it, and you had some understanding of magnetic fields and the connection between wave length and frequency, now playing out audibly before you. The things you learnt in school in physics had a tangible meaning.

And it did us all a great deal of good. Those people who struggled to improve their crystal sets were the ones who went on to improve radio and develop radar, television, and the like.

How did the crystal set work? If you drop a stone in a pool of water, beautiful circular waves propagate outward. Where the stone hits the water, the water level bounces up and down, and it does so at a constant frequency. Some distance from the centre, if there is a leaf floating on the surface, it bobs up and down when the waves reach it with exactly the same frequency but much diminished amplitude.

Radio, or wireless as it was then, is similar. The transmitting station sends out electromagnetic waves. What exactly the medium is that takes the place of the water in the pond is a question best left to the physicists. In earlier times it was called *ether,* or *aether,* a term borrowed from the ancients for that which filled the universe, but nowadays ether is considered

> a hypothetical invisible substance postulated (in older theory) as pervading space and serving as the medium for the transmission of light waves and other forms of radiant energy.[59]

If you ask scientists what has replaced it, their answer will sound like a political statement. Whatever it is, you cannot see it, feel it, or weigh it, and you cannot put some in a bottle to send it to a friend, because it is already there and always has been.

Whatever the medium is, these electromagnetic waves travel through it, and if you hang a copper wire, an aerial, from your bedroom window to a nearby tree, you will pick up these vibrations as a small electric current, although its energy will be minute compared with the waves emitted by the broadcasting station. Two questions arise. One question is, how can we magnify the tiny signal so that it has sufficient strength to produce a sound in our headphones? The other is "How do we separate the signal we want from a particular station from all the other electromagnetic waves from other stations, or perhaps those from a local thunderstorm or even from the ignition of a passing motorcycle?"

To answer these questions, we need to understand the phenomenon of resonance.

In the crystal set, a condenser, made of moveable metal plates, stores electrical charge. It is connected to a coil of copper wire wound on a cardboard cylinder. If there is a charge on the condenser, a current will flow through the coil, discharging the condenser and creating a magnetic field inside the coil. When the current stops, the field will collapse, and the energy in it will charge up the condenser again. It is a vibrating system, just like a child on a swing. With a swing, the oscillations come from the transfer of potential energy to kinetic energy; with the radio, the energy in the condenser is that of static electricity, the kind that makes your hair stand on end if a charged body is near. This is changed to the energy of the magnetic field in the coil.

Very little energy is lost as one changes to the other, and the important thing is that as there is no mass involved, the oscillations can happen very quickly, at many million times a second—megahertz—or if you are very advanced, even faster—gigahertz!

If you adjust the natural frequency of the circuit by moving the condenser plates or only using part of the coil, you can make the frequency of the oscillation of electricity between the coil and condenser exactly match that of the transmitting station. This is known as "tuning," and until recently, you did it by turning a knob on your radio to reach a particular broadcasting station. Nowadays you mostly just press a button, and likely that widely used word will become archaic. When the coil and condenser in your crystal set were tuned, each minutely small impulse received by the aerial will amplify the current, just as many tiny, carefully timed pushes on a child on a swing make it go as high as you dare.

In physics, the phenomenon of small impulses at the right moment building up a large oscillation is known as resonance. The essential feature is that the frequency of the impulses must match the natural frequency of the vibrating system. In the radio, the impulses come so rapidly that the oscillations will build up almost instantaneously.

Now, if you connect your headphones to this resonating circuit, you will hear nothing. One reason is that the frequency is much above the level that the ear can hear; the other is that the headphones would draw the current down to zero. So this is where the "crystal" comes in. The crystals used in crystal sets are naturally occurring diodes. A diode is a device that only transmits current in one direction, preventing the current in the resonator from being drawn away. It has a second function in that the strength of the current going to the headphones is proportional to the strength of the signal transmitted by the station. The station arranges its signals so that the strength or amplitude of the signal being broadcast varies at a lower frequency, one that we can hear. In this way the audio signal, which carries the speech or music, is superimposed on the high frequency carrier wave, which has a fixed frequency for the station we want to receive. And thus, amidst all the electromagnetic signals that surround us, we only receive the one we want. Our set only resonates at the particular frequency of the station we want to hear.

Nowadays amplification of signals and sound is cheap and all too accessible. With the crystal set, you never had quite as much as you wanted. To measure performance, the Q factor was used. In physics and engineering, the term *Q factor* is used to describe the ease with which a system will maintain resonance. A system with a high Q value will resonate freely, whereas a system with a low Q value has a lot of damping or energy loss and requires more energy to achieve and maintain resonance.

You may or may not be interested in the crystal set, but bear in mind that it was a vital link in the evolutionary chain that led to modern communications. Remember too that the key element was the naturally occurring diode, the crystal. The diode is one of the basic elements of modern electronics, but in the days of the crystal set, you could not buy a diode or even make one—they had to be dug up, because the right properties only existed in certain minerals. Surely it is a wonderful thing that the precursor of the modern diode was lying around in the ground, and had been since the world began! It needed a clever person to find the mineral, another to discover its properties, and a third to find out how to use it.

We live in a most incredible workshop, with many plants, minerals, and animals all around us. We can turn them into useful things, or if not useful, they are a source of fun and wonderment. Some may take this as a happy accident. Others have a different view:

> He makes grass to grow for the cattle, and plants for man to cultivate—
>
> bringing forth food from the earth, wine that gladdens the heart of man,
>
> oil to make his face shine, and bread that sustains his heart.
>
> . . .
>
> How many are your works, O Lord! In wisdom you made them all:
>
> the earth is full of your creatures, living things both large and small.
>
> There the ships go to and fro, and the leviathan, which you formed to frolic there.[60]

Beginning in the eighteenth century, scientists in the Western world measured these natural phenomena, discovered new things about them, and set them in a sound framework of understanding. Engineers put this knowledge to useful effect. This was the revolution that changed the world.

But we do not realise that it is quickly running out of steam.

During recent decades there has been enormous progress in computers and information technology, but where are the laboratories that are still exploring the vast storehouse of the natural world? Nowadays you have to say what you will discover before you can obtain funds to look. The result is that much "research" is only dotting i's and crossing t's on things already understood. Furthermore, simulation and modelling have enabled researchers to escape from the discipline of the real world and deal with convenient abstractions.

The result is that we cannot seem to advance beyond the internal combustion engine and its demand for oil for our transport. Our performance in using nuclear energy for electricity production has been poor. We are not controlling water flow and irrigation to keep up with our demands for growth. Our children are learning less and less about the basic physics and chemistry of the natural world and more and more about simulation and virtual existence. Have we, in fact, peaked in our ability to explore the resources of the world and in our ability to provide for the population and the way of life we assume will always be ours?

In talking about our artistic performance—with words that could be said about our engineering and scientific achievements—a writer has put it,

> It is closing time in the gardens of the West and from now on the artist will be judged only by the resonance of his solitude or the quality of his despair.[61]

There is much truth in this, but it is sad.

Let us continue instead to talk about resonance. The crystal set shows how we can use resonance to amplify a tiny signal. What about ourselves? We oscillate. Can we be made to resonate?

DAMPING

Any system that oscillates, be it a tuning fork, the coil and condenser in a crystal set, or the pendulum in a clock, has its own natural frequency, that is, the speed with which it oscillates when free to do so. Small impulses can build up large oscillations in such a system if they are delivered in tune with the natural frequency. This is resonance, whether it is you pushing a child on a swing or an annoying rattle in your car at a certain speed. The question we now ask is whether a person who is pushed and pulled in daily life at just the right frequency will resonate?

You know the answer. If it all seems too horrible, be assured that there is a preventative mechanism, *internal friction,* that drains away some of the energy associated with the swinging to and fro. In engineering, this draining away of energy is known as damping.

One of the amazing people of the last hundred years was Nikola Tesla.[62] He was a prolific inventor, a brilliant scientist and engineer, and probably a little mad. Without wishing to diminish a good effort,[63] we can say that he has lacked the right kind of biographer. He is poorly understood by the scientific community, and yet one of his inventions is the cornerstone of our use of electricity today.[64] Another, lesser known idea of his, which was not quite right, was that he could destroy any building by determining its natural frequency and giving it small and repeated pushes at just the right moment—like pushing the child on the swing—until the oscillations became so great that it fell down.

Being a little strange, Tesla experimented on the apartment building he lived in, and while it did not fall down, he did manage to produce sufficient vibration to be threatened with eviction! What saved him and the building was that the internal friction of the concrete and bricks in the building, the *damping,* was greater than the energy he could put in with his small repeated pushes. Fortunately for Tesla's neighbours, the building they lived in had a low Q value.

Tesla had an extraordinary understanding of the physical world, but his understanding of people was weak. Had he applied his analytical power to people, he might be better remembered today. We too have our damping, and like our natural frequency it is an individual characteristic that differs greatly from person to person. Some have very little internal friction and easily become excited; they are not easy to live with. Others are more heavily damped, and their mood swings are small. It is tempting to suggest that we should rate people in terms of their Q factor: we could dismiss the terms *hyperactive* and *restless* and say they suffer from a high Q. We often admire people because of their imperturbability (low Q factor) and say that they are always the same. This may not be completely true.

> Even constancy itself is no other but a slower and more languishing motion.[65]

It used to be fashionable to describe people's characteristics in colourful ways. A "highly strung" person was like a piano string and vibrated all the time; the opposite personality was called languid, or more directly, phlegmatic. Even in our affections for others we have our swings. We are never constant. We veer at one moment toward infatuation and a little later swing the other way, if not to loathing, at least to a state of mild annoyance.

More robustly, Shakespeare makes clear the hazard of too violent an attachment. In *Twelfth Night*, Duke Orsino is clearly smitten:

> O! when mine eyes did see Olivia first,
>
> Methought she purged the air of pestilence.

But the duke is wise enough to know that this state is neither desirable nor long-lasting!

> O spirit of love! how quick and fresh art thou,
>
> That, notwithstanding thy capacity
>
> Receiveth as the sea, nought enters there
>
> Of what validity and pitch soe'er
>
> But falls into abatement and low price,
>
> Even in a minute.[66]

Shakespeare reminds us of how quickly we can swing from one extreme to another. In our infatuation, we delight in being part of another person and knowing the other's thoughts intimately, but suddenly we can move to the other extreme where we say to ourselves, "I know exactly what he or she is about to say, I am waiting for it, and I cannot bear to hear it!"

The greatest difference between each of us as individuals lies in the frequency of our natural vibrations and the extent of our internal damping. These determine our response to the stimuli imposed on us. If we are prodded with diabolical cleverness at just the right frequency, we can be made to resonate.

George Orwell[67] and others show how we can be manipulated by modern communications and how a majority of a country or state may act on premises that they know to be false just because they have been pushed by a cunning campaign. Most telling of all, we can see that the impulses in life do not have to be strong to motivate us. They must simply have the right rhythm.

AVOIDING RESONANCE

The engineer is trained to avoid unwanted resonance. The trick is to know the natural frequency of each part of the design and ensure that no one part can excite another. An example is the engine and propeller shaft of a boat. Each will have its own natural frequency of vibration. The engine driving the propeller will not deliver a smooth torque, but one that fluctuates because of the explosions in the cylinders that create the power. One must ensure that the frequency of the torque variations in the two systems, the one being the engine and the other being the shaft and propeller, are quite different from each other. If they are the same, the one will excite the other, and noise and vibration will build up even to a destructive level.

An example that we can easily study is the domestic clothes washing machine. On the spin cycle, the clothes and tub spin at a high speed to remove the water; inevitably the clothes and the tub will not be exactly balanced, so there will be an excitation at the spin speed. What we must avoid is this excitation causing a large vibration of the tub. How is this accomplished? If you make sure your machine is empty and disconnected from the power source, you can determine the natural frequency of the tub suspension yourself by moving the tub sideways with your hand, then releasing it. You will find that the suspension is very flexible and that the tub naturally oscillates at a low frequency. It is also highly damped and returns to rest very quickly. In operation, the tub and its load accelerate rapidly through the speed corresponding with the natural frequency of the suspension, and resonance does not have a chance to build up. At full speed the excitation due to an out-of-balance load has a much greater frequency than that of the suspension and cannot excite the tub to large oscillations.

This sounds fine, but we know it does not always work. Sometimes if the load is too much out of balance, the machine cannot accelerate quickly through this so-called critical frequency, and the tub vibrates alarmingly. The makers of washing machines have incorporated a sensor to detect this which will shut down the machine. We are given a very clear instruction: if your washing machine starts jumping around,

SWITCH OFF AND REDISTRIBUTE THE LOAD

This is exactly the advice Isaiah gave to his people thousands of years ago. Why is it that we follow instructions with our washing machines, but not in our daily lives? The proverbial advice is:

> If obstinacy does not work the first time, try something else!

If our lives start to vibrate out of control, we should switch off and rearrange things, but our obstinacy stops us doing this.

CONCLUSION

We see that, like many physical systems, people can be stirred up by small and perhaps unseen signals, ones that are delivered at just the right frequency. Fortunately, as individuals, we respond to different frequencies, so that we do not all jump up and down in unison—although it is true that mass hysteria does happen from time to time with certain groups.

It has often been said that the world is only changed by people who are different, or, to say it another way, by *unreasonable* individuals. It may be that these are ones who just happen to have a different natural frequency. We all have people like that near us; perhaps we should be thankful for them.

> If a man does not keep pace with his companions, perhaps it is because he hears a different drummer. Let him step to the music which he hears, however measured or far away.[68]

In terms of what has been described, perhaps these people are just tuned in to a different channel—and what is wrong with that?

Chapter 6
CONTROL

"control, vt. to operate or regulate ...
to hold back; curb, restrain."
—Webster's New World Dictionary

The control of machines has become such a large subject that it is now a separate branch of engineering. What it involves is clear from the name, but the complexity and the extent of the subject is rarely appreciated. At its simplest level, we all understand it. The control part of a light is the switch. Turn it on, and the light comes on. Technically, this is known as "on-off" control. A bit more advanced is the control of the gearbox in a car, where the driver manipulates the clutch, gear lever, and accelerator to get the car up a hill. This is known as "manual control," though manual transmissions have now been largely replaced by the automatic transmission.

A vast amount of clever engineering has been required to bring these controls to perfection, and in a car, the automatic gearbox or transmission has become invisible and, by St Expury's rule, out of mind. But think for a moment. You have an engine. You as the driver determine how much power you want to apply by pressing the accelerator (or gas pedal, depending where you live). The system must know the car's speed so it can select the right gear and decide when to change gears, and on top of this, a device is needed to actually shift the gears.

The gears, shafts, and cylinders involved have all been designed by mechanical engineers. Getting them all to work *together* is the province of control engineers.

If you follow the history of the gearbox, a device which we now take for granted, you will find that it took about fifty years from the time people first tried it until it was finally successful, economical, and as we have said, put out of mind.

This is only one example of control engineering.

Nowadays a complete oil refinery, with all its pumps, valves, and vessels, can be controlled by a vast system employing many computers and very few people.

The basis of control engineering can be put briefly, although the experts would consider this an oversimplification. There are three essentials parts. The system must be instrumented so that at any instant you, or more precisely the system, knows where it is—the *state* of the system. You must then know where you want to be—the *set point*—and finally you must have a mechanism to adjust the system so that it moves toward the desired operating condition. The difference between where you are and where you should be is called the *error,* and the magnitude of the error determines the speed of adjustment.

To go beyond this explanation we must venture into the control textbooks, but you can see already that something similar occurs in everyday life. A young mother whose busy children were engaged in many activities—football, ballet, horse-riding and so on, said in a letter,

> I seem to spend my whole life going from where I am to where I ought to be![69]

Her control system was not quite coping. We all know the feeling!

Philosophers have long puzzled over our habit of wandering from the proper path and how we are brought back to it, although they did not think about it as a control problem. More than two thousand years ago Aristotle[70] suggested that for any one human behaviour there are two opposite and undesirable extremes; he labelled these as vices. In the middle was a desirable mean that he considered as virtue. Something draws us back to the mean. In engineering we would call it an error-correcting mechanism.

TABLE OF VIRTUES AND VICES

Sphere of action	Excess	Mean	Deficiency
Fear	cowardice	courage	rashness
Pleasure	licentiousness	temperance	insensibility
Honour	vanity	magnanimity	pusillanimity
Anger	irascibility	patience	lack of spirit

In the millennia since Aristotle, philosophers have debated what it is that draws humans back toward the virtuous mean. The cynic may say that judging by most human behaviour the mechanism is rather defective, but to be fair, we could be worse. In control engineering, the speed with which you correct the error is important. If the correction is too slow, the system is always lagging behind where it should be. If it is too high, the correction will overshoot the mark, then reverse and overshoot in the opposite direction. The system will oscillate about the desired setting and is said to be "hunting."

People may also have ill-adjusted control systems. To some, things are never quite right, and they correct the smallest errors (and drive everyone to distraction). Others are simply sluggish and never quite where they should be. Confucius recognized this long ago:

> The Master said, "If I cannot get men who steer a middle course to associate with, I would rather have the impetuous and the hasty. For the impetuous at least assert themselves; and the hasty have this at least to be said for them, that there are things they leave undone."[71]

He did not have time for those who were too particular:

> Ji Wen used to think thrice before acting. The Master hearing of it said, "Twice is quite enough."[72]

The more one reads the Analects, the more one feels that the Master must have been fun to be near. Nowadays the rule is that:

> A civil servant doesn't make jokes.[73]

and our world becomes increasingly boring! During part of his life, Confucius was a civil servant, but clearly not a typical one.

One possible force driving us toward the middle, "virtuous" state is that we wish to look good in the eyes of those around us. In the long run, this is not a good control mechanism; our neighbours may be wrong about what is good, or we could easily be seen as ridiculous. Again:

> The Master said, "[The good man] does not grieve that other people do not recognize his

merits. His only anxiety is lest he should fail to recognize theirs."[74]

CONSTANCY

We need control systems in engineering because our machines can never be set and left to operate without one; they will drift off the set point. The same is true with us. We will not correct our errors without being directed by some intuition, belief, faith, or doctrine. Even then, constancy is more an ideal than an actuality, which, like Caesar, we see in ourselves but not in others:

> I am constant as the northern star,
>
> Of whose true-fixed and resting quality,
>
> There is no fellow in the firmament.
>
> . . .
>
> Yet in the number I do know but one,
>
> That unassailable holds that rank,
>
> Unshaked of motion: and that I am he.[75]

Caesar had a number of virtues, but modesty was not one of them. Shakespeare was perhaps right to imagine him saying this. On the other hand, to talk about yourself, no matter what you say, is not a clever idea, Montaigne warns us. If we say bad things about ourselves, everybody will believe us; while if we extol our virtues, nobody will believe us! Montaigne considered constancy, or the lack of it, as worthy of careful examination:

> It is a hard matter from all antiquity, to pick out a dozen men who have formed their lives to one certain and constant course, which is the principle of wisdom.[76]

He quotes Seneca:

> Esteem it a great thing always to act as one and the same man.[77]

Seneca praises a friend for being constant:

> You do not tear from place to place and unsettle yourself with one move after another. Restlessness of that sort is symptomatic of a sick mind. Nothing, to my way of thinking, is a better proof of a well-ordered mind than man's ability to stop just where he is and pass some time in his own company.[78]

Pascal had similar thoughts:

> All the misfortunes of men derive from one
> single thing, which is their inability to be at
> ease [alone] in a room.[79]

We long for a world in which our friends would be the same yesterday, today, and tomorrow and where life would stick to the straight and narrow path, but we know the reality is perpetual oscillation. We, like controlled machines, are never static but always moving to and fro about our set point; our equilibrium is dynamic, and we need some system to keep it where it should be.

In recent years engineers have been able to incorporate computers into the control loop, and this has expanded the capability of their systems. Our brains are part of the control mechanism that brings us back to where we ought to be, or at least we hope they are. If so, then, as each of us has a brain that is unique, each person will have different dynamics to bring him back to his set point.

The wise person observes these differences carefully and is better able to judge how an individual will respond to a situation. The world of robotic and computer-controlled systems is expanding rapidly, and as it does, we will better understand control both in physical processes and, perhaps, in ourselves.

LOAD MATCHING

The engineering theory involved in coupling an engine or prime mover so that it drives a device to do some job is called "load matching," and it is part of control theory. In developing design skills in students, it is sometimes permissible to devise traps that the student can fall into so that you can reinforce the learning experience as you help them dig themselves out of the hole. It would seem, for example, that if you have to choose a drive for a fan that absorbs 8 horsepower and you choose a motor of 10 horsepower, that is all you have to do. Wrong. Students will almost inevitably fall into a hole in matching a driver to a load. Unless you consider all that may happen from starting up running at full speed and then shutting down, you have not fulfilled the design requirements.

Perhaps the closest analogy to this engineering problem of matching loads is the institution of marriage. The modern world tends to neglect and underestimate the long history and development of marriage, and yet it is perhaps one of the most important aspects of civilisation. Historically, marriage has been a mechanism for sharing the loads arising from building a home and raising a family; one partner will be the engine for one task, while in another task the roles are reversed. The idea that each partner should perform equal and identical roles is of recent invention, and obviously, biology prevents it being perfectly achieved.

The importance of the institution is too often overlooked. Montaigne had no doubt:

> Let us take that which is most necessary and profitable for human society; it will be marriage . . . [80]

The Book of Common Prayer has been an influential text for three centuries (and is also beautifully written). It gives the reason for marriage

> It was ordained for the mutual society, help, and comfort, that the one ought to have of

the other, both in prosperity and adversity.[81]

and is quite explicit. It states that marriage

is not by any to be enterprized, or taken in
hand, unadvisedly, lightly or wantonly, to
satisfy men's carnal lusts and appetites, like
brute beasts that have no understanding; but
reverently, discreetly, advisedly, soberly, and
in the fear of God.[82]

The form of the marriage service that contains
these words is rarely used nowadays. Perhaps we are
less tolerant of plain speaking than our forefathers.

Literature abounds with examination of marriages; few reach the heights of Jane Austen's writing.

The happiest existing marriage in all Austen's
novels (as distinct from those with which they,
hopefully, end) is that of the Crofts . . . [83]

On his quarterdeck, Admiral Croft no doubt
controlled his fleet with skill and precision, but on
land, driving his wife in a horse and gig, it was a
different matter. His wife bravely endured his driv-

ing but was ever on the alert and avoided disaster by small, unnoticed interventions. Jane Austen captures the whole marriage in a short paragraph about a near-encounter with a gatepost.

> "My dear Admiral, that post!—we shall certainly take that post."
>
> But by coolly giving the reins a better direction herself they happily passed the danger; and by once afterwards judiciously putting out her hand they neither fell into a rut, or ran foul of a dung-cart; and Anne, with some amusement at their style of driving, which she imagined no bad representation of the general guidance of their affairs, found herself safely deposited by them at the Cottage.[84]

That one partner can intervene without drawing attention and that the other can accept correction without offence is one of the smaller miracles that happens in a successful marriage.

A writer often quoted at weddings is Kahlil Gibran, a twentieth-century Persian poet and philosopher. His work has reached hundreds of thousands, if not millions, though he has been totally ignored or castigated by the philosophical establishment. While it is true that some parts of his work are not of a high standard, some things resonate. On marriage he says:

> Let there be spaces in your togetherness.
>
> And let the winds of heaven dance between you.
>
> . . .
>
> And stand together yet not too near together:
>
> For pillars of the temple stand apart. [85]

Space in a marriage involves the dimensions of both time and distance. We all need time alone and time with our friends, and most yearn for a corner we can call our own. Husband and wife who are too close in their affections may have children who feel left out. At the other extreme, the dangers of lengthy separation are well known, and experience often shows it is untrue that "absence makes the heart grow fonder." The idea of standing apart as columns in the temple has a good ring. Parents must always stretch out their arms and provide shelter and protection for their children.

Gibran was also aware that we fluctuate and are never steady:

> Verily you are suspended like scales between your sorrow and your joy.
>
> Only when you are empty are you at a standstill and balanced.[86]

If the world is not right at the moment, give it time to move back to a better place. Remember that there is a control system of some kind operating in our daily lives. It is good to understand it and respect it.

Chapter 7
CREATIVITY (AND ITS FOES)

"In creating, the only hard thing is to begin."
—James Russell Lowell

Engineering design is a creative activity, as is all design. The difference between it and other creative disciplines is the constraint under which the engineer works. The artist is constrained only by the size of the canvas and the requirement that the paint must not flake off or fade away. The engineer is constrained by all the physical laws governing the strength of materials and the laws of mechanics. Well-established rules govern the application of scientific and empirical knowledge, and the engineer must always provide a proof that what is designed will work—not *might* work, not *should* work, but *will* work.

"Has the engineer shown that the design will work?" This is the criteria we use to determine whether a design is satisfactory, but when we to try to rank designs in some order of merit, the yardstick is usually the extent to which they exhibit creativity.

This measure is not limited to the world of engineering. We all know that those historical times when mankind made great social progress were also times when creativity flourished. The Renaissance was filled with innovation in the arts, science, and literature; many wondrous new machines and devices appeared during the industrial revolution in the nineteenth century. Toward the end of the twentieth century, incredible progress was made in electronic communications and computation.

We automatically associate creativity with the advance of our society and improvement in our economic well-being. It is not surprising, therefore, that when things are not going so well for a nation, or for a company or indeed any enterprise, we hear a call for *a more creative approach*. We look for creativity, but all too often we cannot find it. It has a very elusive nature. The nuclear physicists have similar problems with their tiny particles. In their attempt to corner them, they invent strange constructions like Heisenberg's uncertainty principle.[87] Those who look for the source from which creativity springs soon discover a similar need. The harder you search for the origins of creativity, the more they just aren't there!

Arthur Koestler[88] wrestled with this problem, and although it is some years now since his work, *The Act of Creation*,[89] was published, it contains some excellent leads. He makes the useful connection between the sudden flash of invention, "the Eureka moment," and the reason we laugh at a joke. The comedian carefully leads us into a situation and makes us feel clever that we have worked out what is happening and that we fully understand the scene. Suddenly, he tears away the veil, and we all see that it is quite different from what we thought. Laughter is the automatic response to this shock to the senses.

The act of invention is similar. There is an existing view or explanation for a certain process that we all accept because that is what we have been told. Then someone wanders away a little from conventional thinking and examines and worries over the current concept. Suddenly it is all seen in a different light, and the discoverer has a better explanation, one in which all the pieces fit together more harmoniously. Often things previously thought to be separate and unrelated are now seen as part of a wider and more embracing whole.

We have all had these flashes of inspiration. For most of us, they are only little, unlikely to win us a Nobel Prize. The experience is often silent and solitary, but it is akin to laughter. The tension we felt at not being able to connect and explain a certain set of events as well as we might is suddenly relieved and replaced with tranquillity and well-being. The thought that is uppermost in our mind is, *Yes, that is right!*

Of course, not all creative activities culminate in this sudden burst of awareness. Often we plod along and enter into a new invention by small steps, but we finish with a clearer picture where, bit by bit, the pieces fit together to create a new and bigger picture.

A pragmatic way of dealing with creativity is to accept that we do not know where the ideas come from and that we have a poor understanding of the mechanics of the creative process. What we can do is ask, "How can we prepare ourselves so that we can be creative when the chance arises?" Perhaps Confucius had the answer with his thought, earlier quoted in chapter 3:

> He who learns but does not think is lost. He who thinks but does not learn is in great danger.[90]

If we want to be creative in a particular field, we must *learn* and master that field. This is what education is all about. To extend your knowledge of something, you must be at least a competent performer in that particular field.

It is here that I suspect some of our ideas about early education are wrong. It has become fashionable in education to put the acquisition of knowledge into second place behind a vaguely defined objective of developing one's ability to think, to innovate, to express oneself, and so on. More than

150 years ago, Dickens laughed at Mr Gadgrind, who was only concerned with "facts":

> Now what I want is, Facts . . . Facts alone are wanted in life.[91]

Perhaps we should now make fun of the educationalists who want children to concentrate on "self-expression" before they have mastered the basic words and grammar to express themselves! If you engage young children in a serious conversation, you will find their appetite for facts is insatiable. They love them—and what is wrong with that? It is true that Mr Gadgrind's "facts" are only a beginning, but so also is childhood.

The great mathematician, Poincaré, wrote on the philosophy of science and said:

> Science is built up of facts, as a house is built of stones; but an accumulation of facts is no more a science than a heap of stones is a house.[92]

This is true, but try to build a house without a pile of stones, bricks, or timber! It cannot be done.

Nowadays our knowledge of the natural world is so large that to understand even a small part of it requires considerable learning, but this cannot be avoided, and the best time to start learning is when we are young. A wise musician, on being asked his advice for the younger person, had only one recommendation. It was to acquire a large repertoire as soon as possible. Get the notes of many works into your brain while you have the learning ability of a child, because childhood is a fleeting opportunity. Do not be so concerned about interpretation and appreciation—that will come later.

The computer may provide us with a useful analogy. The first thing we do with a new computer is to load the software. This includes a dictionary, a mathematical processor, a file storage system, an operating system and much more. Your operating system stores a vast number of facts, but can it be made to create anything on its own? No. Left to itself, your computer cannot write a book. You must create the characters and devise the plot. Your computer can be a great help when you create something, but to do so it must be loaded with facts and operating systems. Like the child, learn the facts and master the techniques first, then create. Let us accept the example of that which has been shown to work.

Koestler, in trying to understand the operating system for creativity, was also aware of the importance of facts:

> Without the hard little bits of marble which are called "facts" or "data" one cannot compose a mosaic; what matters, however, are not so much the individual bits, but the successive patterns into which you arrange them, then break them up and rearrange them.[93]

The facts are like Poincaré's heap of stones. It is true that the new picture, the mosaic, is the important thing and is what we are striving for, but let us not forget that the building blocks are also essential. At least with children, we will not be depriving them of any opportunity if we help them do what they are best suited to do and what they enjoy doing, namely acquiring facts and data. Later on they can compose a new mosaic.

Learning is a slow operation, and it would be

good if we could short-circuit the process and learn creativity directly. Given the similarity between humour and inventiveness, one could ask if there are schools for comedians? Koestler thought there was no shortcut.

> Creative activity could be described as a type of learning process where teacher and pupil are located in the same individual.[94]

We have to acquire this creative ability ourselves. Nobody can do it for us. It is true that some schools of design, or some research institutes, or Edison's famous Menlo Park and perhaps some recent high-tech laboratories, have existed in which creativity flourished. The common feature in them all was a free and financed opportunity to explore and an understanding of what was needed. Efforts to understand the *modus operandi* of the creative process itself have been unsuccessful. We can prepare the ground for innovation and creativity, but beyond that we can only hope.

Given the need to understand a particular subject before we can expand it, it is not surprising that we see there is more creativity in emerging fields where one can become familiar with the existing body of knowledge reasonably quickly. An example is electronic computation and data processing. Innovation in computers, mobile phones, and the like has been prodigious in recent decades, perhaps because it is easier to bring oneself to the point where one can invent here than in other fields. Creative people with their eye on the main chance have been quick to move into these newer fields; whether mankind is well served by this concentration on new technologies and a perceived lack of interest in the more established areas is for you to decide.

The popular opinion is that there is always a demand for more creativity, but unfortunately it is rarely there when we want it. The laws of supply and demand do not seem to work, and many of us feel there is an undersupply.

Although we do not know how and where creativity arises, as we have seen, there is much we can do to create the right conditions. The gardener cannot make seeds germinate, but he can prepare the ground well and plant the seeds at the right time to ensure that they will flourish. This being the case, and knowing that we would be better off if our society was more creative, we should be able to open the floodgates, as has happened from time to time in the past, but we are not doing this now. *Why not?* One reason, and this is a bit of a guilty secret, is that not all those who profess to be on the side of creativity truly want to see it flourish. Worse, some will undermine it if they see it developing. *Why?* The reason, as has been said in various ways by many over the ages, is this:

Creativity is the enemy of the status quo!

This is not a new idea. More than three hundred years ago, Montaigne, who understood well how states and governments operate, said:

The world is unapt to be cured; and so impatient of anything that presses it, that it thinks of nothing but disengaging itself at whatever price . . . Nothing presses so hard upon a state as innovation: change only gives form to injustice and tyranny.[95]

The same applies to industry. There are good examples of companies that have invested heavily in product development, in better ways of manufacturing, and have done well, yet other companies turn their backs on doing the same. One reason is found in corporate evolution. Many enterprises were started by people who had invented a new product, process, or system. These were creative people, but eventually they retired or died. Their place was keenly sought by those who wanted the prestige or income of the position but were not, themselves, creative. Once there, these people worked hard to defend their position. They realised that if things changed too much, they could be in danger. They sensed greater security in the status quo. Innovation was something to keep under control.

This habit of those in authority defending the status quo is not confined to industry. It happens in any organisation, be it a local tennis club, a research committee, or a political party. There are always people who defend their power to decide by making sure that it is not endangered by innovation, creative activities, or new ways of doing things. Perhaps we are hardwired to behave like this, and it is a built-in safety mechanism. If this is so, then thinking about something in a different way, building something that no one else has made before, finding a solution that others did not find, doing any of these things is, by definition, being *unreasonable*. George Bernard Shaw long maintained that the world was only changed by unreasonable people. Perhaps we should accept that in being creative, we are always in a way being unreasonable.

JK Galbraith, in describing the modern world as "a time when the bland lead the bland," said that nowadays:

> the man of controversy is looked upon as a disturbing influence;
>
> . . . originality is taken to be a mark of instability. [96]

As social animals we avoid being unpopular, but if we realise that there will be opposition and understand the reason for it, we can brave the current, swim against the tide, be unreasonable and difficult, and enjoy the rewards of creativity. Unpopularity is a fickle thing, after all, and opinions change.

In the 1930s, the director of a major public art gallery in Australia refused to allow an exhibition of Impressionist art on the grounds that it was trivial and decadent. The price of a single Monet today proves that we now think differently. Fortunately, creative people are not greatly influenced by popular opinion. The joys of creativity are many and more than enough to compensate for a little opposition.

Interestingly, creative people do not know where their ideas come from any more than the rest of us do. Henry Ford, when asked the question, said, "I don't know. I just snatch them out of the air as they fly past." Ford was a perennial deceiver, but it's probable he told the truth here, and his answer is as good as we will get from any great inventor. Any attempt to analyse the source of creativity leads us to a lot of negatives. On the other hand, we have the deep conviction that, as humans, we cannot stand still. We must change, invent, and progress. We should not allow our minds to be deflected away from this by opposition.

Again, Montaigne helps us to understand. He reminds us that there will always be structures in our lives, in our jobs, our associations, our clubs, and at the highest levels, in our state. We are obliged to show respect for those in authority in our outward behaviour, but what we think—what goes on in our minds—is a different matter!

> That which I myself adore in kings is the crowd of adorers; all reverence and submission are due to them, except that of the understanding: my reason is not obliged to bow and bend: my knees are.[97]

We are all free to think the new thought. We can all invent a novel device, and we can all create in our minds a new system. Fortunately, most of us live in countries where we can express these ideas without fear. We should expect opposition and we can understand its source, but we are free to be creative.

A wonderful thing about the ability to invent and create is that it is always with us and does not diminish with age. The popular idea is that inventiveness is a young person's game, but this is not true. Writers, composers, artists (Picasso and many others), and designers go on to a prodigious age. It is true that amongst younger people, a greater proportion are creative than is the case amongst older people; this is because, in the course of life, many creative people are lured into positions where they are required to defend the status quo. They defect, and the numbers left in the creative ranks are consequently diminished. In Montaigne's terms, they have bent the mind as well as the knee!

If you are creative now, keep at it. Creativity is the virtuous and rewarding path. Keep at it, because your ability will stay with you even as you age. It is like Cleopatra's allure:

Age cannot wither her, nor custom stale

Her infinite variety. [98]

Chapter 8
ENVOY

*"'Where shall I begin, please your Majesty?' he asked.
'Begin at the beginning,' the King said, gravely,
'and go on till you come to the end; then stop.'"*
—Lewis Carroll, *Alice's Adventures in Wonderland*

When we look at the ways of the financial community and the many things they do that may be legal but are clearly immoral, when we see the outright deceit of political leaders, when we are appalled at the situation with health care or feel deeply concerned about the evils of globalisation, we could easily reach the despair of the psalmist:

> But for me, my feet were almost gone; my steps had well nigh slipped.

For I was envious at the foolish, when I saw
the prosperity of the wicked.[99]

Contemplation of where our world is and where it might be heading gives weight to Connolly's fear, already mentioned: "It is closing time in the gardens of the West."[100] And yet! And yet we live in an amazingly rich and plentiful world.

One hundred years ago, one had to be well up the economic scale to afford a horse and trap; now it seems that everyone has an automobile. With the advances in aviation, most can afford journeys that would have seemed impossible less than a century ago. Communication has so improved that we can talk to a loved one on the other side of the globe, instantly, live and visible, for very little cost.

These things have all been achieved by invention and technology, and they not only expand our lives but are conducted with remarkable safety. When I was young, my parents would never travel together on the same plane, on the grounds that if there was an accident we would be left as orphans. That idea would now be seen as quaint or just ridiculous. The reason we can feel this way lies with the standards of the engineering profession and the conditions under which design is performed. If governments dismantle or underfund the agencies required to preserve safety, not only in the air, but in our roads and bridges and in our public health systems, or if engineers relax their standards, accidents will start to proliferate.

In looking at our behaviour as human beings, the most obvious thing is that we are never static or at rest. We are constantly on the move.

> We fluctuate betwixt various inclinations; we will nothing freely, nothing absolutely, nothing constantly.[101]

Engineers are accustomed to dealing with dynamic and vibrating systems, and it is not surprising that engineering concepts can be applied to each of us as well as to machines. We have our individual natural frequency, we resonate, and as long as we take it all in a light-hearted way, we can apply engineering control theory in dealing with those about us. It is not an outrageous proposal to say that we can be considered as the product of a design process that is close to that which engineers use to design their machines—hence the title of this book.

Some philosophers or theologians have accepted divine creation:

> God made no tools for himself, he needs none; he created for himself a partner in the dialogue of time, and one who is capable of holding converse. [102]

but even these proponents feel that we still have a long way to go:

> God himself . . . awaits man's help and contribution towards Creation. But we, instead of turning towards him his own image in ourselves and offering him freely the fruits of our creative strength, have wasted and squandered that strength in superficial self-affirmation.[103]

In our history we have known times when our creative strength was fruitful, but it seems not to be so now. We have largely squandered the opportunity to live productive, caring, and peaceful lives. We obviously need to preserve our creativity, encourage it, and direct it toward the right goals.

If you do not believe in divine design, the idea that we are the result of a design process similar to that of engineering is still a useful working hypothesis. It will help you understand our foibles and habits, and it does work! If you choose to think of those about you as pendulums, you can work out when to nudge them and when to let them swing freely. (It is probably best not to tell them you are doing this!)

Whatever our beliefs, we should remember that we far outstrip any man-made machine in one quality—the ability to imagine, to invent, to create, and to think new thoughts. This is a wonderful possession. Let us cherish it, use it, and make it grow. Remember too that creative ability continues to go on and does not diminish with age. The book of Proverbs tells us that if we follow the right path, the light will not become dim as we grow older as if we were approaching twilight, but rather life will become brighter as in the morning when the day is beginning:

The path of the righteous is like the first gleam of dawn,

shining ever brighter till the full light of day.[104]

The same is true for the bold, the inventive and the creative person.

APPENDIX:
R.R. Whyte: 1910–2002, MBE, BE, FIMech.E.

The author has asked me to contribute this note on my father, Roger Robert Whyte, because the inspiration for this book and many of the ideas came from him. He was the author of two important books published by the Institution of Mechanical Engineers, London: Engineering Progress Through Trouble, 1976, *and* Engineering Progress Through Development, 1980. *His experiences in and contributions to mechanical engineering during the second half of the 20th century were remarkable.*—Robert Whyte, January 2016

Roger Robert Whyte was born in London in 1910, and after struggling with dyslexia in his early schooling, found his vocation in mechanical engineering and mathematics and obtained 1st Class Honours in Mechanical Engineering at Imperial College, London. After graduating, he "had a year out" (in modern parlance) and spent six months living with a family in Freiburg, Germany, followed by six months in Czechoslovakia working in a factory. This gave him a strong foundation in both the German language and their engineering customs, a foundation which lasted all his life. It is interesting to note that the friendship with the German family followed a relationship established by his parents before the First World War and survived the Second World War; the two families are still in contact today.

On his return from Germany he headed to Manchester to start a graduate apprenticeship with the leading engineering firm of the day, Metropolitan Vickers (MV). At MV he specialised in the building of steam turbines, for which there was a burgeoning demand thanks to the need for electrical power generation.

At the outset of the Second World War, the Royal Air Force recognised the need for an axial flow jet engine and to that end sponsored a collaboration between Rolls Royce Aero Engines and MV, firstly to develop a compressor that would be suitable for such an engine and then a full flying engine. At the age of just thirty, RRW was already a leader among his peers in MV and had the engineering acumen, the leadership skills, and the key knowledge of how to make turbine blades needed to become a leading figure in the joint development team, which was located well away from the sprawling MV Trafford Park site in Cheshire.

The years developing the first axial flow jet engine were pivotal for RRW; they gave him a lifelong belief that leaders needed to cut their teeth in demanding positions early in life. The project was highly successful, and the engine they developed ultimately became the Sapphire; it was built in the hundreds in both the USA and the UK. The project was not without its low points. The second engine to fly, mounted in the tail of a Lancaster bomber as a test bed, exploded in flight with the loss of the pilot, and even forty years later when discussing the subject, RRW was visibly upset.

One can only imagine the challenges involved in making highly complex prototypes of turbine blades for a design one thousand times lighter than a traditional steam turbine in a factory that, at the same time, was running absolutely flat-out making items for the war effort. The development of first the compressor and then the engine itself, and the ground-breaking work overcoming stalling problems when quickly going to full throttle, are well documented in RRW's Engineering Progress through Trouble.

In the late 1940s, MV had to decide whether to go into the jet engine business. It was a very sad day for RRW when they decided to concentrate on their core steam turbine business and transfer the technology developed to Rolls Royce. He ensured that all his team secured good positions in Rolls Royce, with a few staying with him in MV. It is not clear why he did not go to Rolls Royce himself, but certainly at the time he had strong roots in Manchester and MV.

Over the next years while building ever larger steam turbines, mainly for what would become the CEGB (Central Electricity Generating Board), RRW was appointed factory superintendent, then factory manager, ultimately running factories in both Manchester and Larne in Northern Ireland. What RRW brought to MV, which by this time had become AEI, was an in-depth knowledge of how highly complex and high-power engineering elements were made. He always had a fascination with making things and in machine tools, and this was an area in which he had a unique knowledge. He was always equipped with a six-inch slide rule in his top pocket and a twelve-inch scientific slide rule on his desk; his note paper was quarter-inch graph paper for technical sketches. In the area of visualisation of mechanical objects he had an almost photographic memory and was of course highly numerate. When it came to the written word he knew his weaknesses and relied heavily on a first-class secretary.

A key point in RRW's career was reached in the 1960s when the CEGB decided that for their next tranche of power stations they would move from the current 100 megawatt (MW) gas turbines to 500MW units. At this stage, no 500MW units were in development, nor were there even any plans to approach this step-by-step; the normal iterative development would have been to build to 200MW and then 400MW units and learn on the way. When AEI pushed back against the CEGB and pressured for a more conventional approach, they were told that if they wanted they could choose not to bid for the 500MW units and step out of the business.

History tells us now that this cavalier approach by the CEGB cost them and their suppliers dearly and seriously damaged those businesses making turbines for them. The problems with these turbines started in development and carried on through manufacturing and on throughout the life of these machines for twenty to thirty years. RRW took a heavy responsibility for both the performance of the units and the financial outcome of the division. In the end, it was time to look for another job. He was quickly snapped up by English Electric Diesels to be their director of engineering with responsibility for six manufacturing sites around the UK. He enjoyed his time, although he missed some of the turbine technology on which he had spent most of his career.

Some years later, as a result of high-level changes and reorganisation in both English Electric and AEI, RRW had to find a new role. He took the loss of day-to-day contact with skilled engineers and with manufacturing with some sadness, but it was, arguably, very good for him in the long run. His old colleagues in the industry quickly came to his support, and in no time at all his week was filled with consulting, lecturing, and book writing, and this continued into his seventies. "Do you know they have asked me to teach that MSc course at the university for another year?" he said in his late seventies with a big smile.

There are few people who experienced at first hand the exciting period of engineering design and development that RRW did. He left a legacy in his description and interpretation of this in his books. His achievements as an engineer were great, but perhaps of equal importance was his trust in the established ethics of the engineering profession, his care and concern for those who worked for him, his fortitude when times were tough, and above all his personal integrity, which never wavered.

Robert Whyte, January 2016

ENDNOTES

1. Psalm: 8
2. Montaigne, 1533 to 1592, Bk. I, Ch.1.
3. Orwell and Politics, Peter Davies, Ed. Penguin Books, 2001, p. 95
4. Henry Ford,1863–1947.
5. Rudyard Kipling, 1865–1936, "The English Flag" (1892).
6. Wm. Wordsworth, 1770–1850, "A Poet's Epitaph."
7. Just So Stories (1902)
8. Henry IV Part I, (1597)
9. Psalm 100
10. How the Scots Invented the Modern World, A Herman, Three Rivers Press, NY, 2001, p.311
11. Dorothy Parker, 1893-1967' "A Pig's Eye View of Literature" 1937.
12. W S Gilbert, 1836-1911, "Princess Ida".
13. Sir Arthur Sullivan, 1842-1900, English composer.
14. 'The Gondoliers' (1889)
15. Friedrich Nietzsche, 1844-1900, "Der Antichrist".
16. Robert Burns, 1759-1796, Green Grow the Rushes, O.
17. Arthur Koestler, 1905-83, "The Ghost in the Machine"
18. A A Milne, 1882-1956.
19. American cartoonist Walt Kelly
20. Oscar Wilde, The Ballad of Reading Gaol
21. Job 5:7. The speaker, Eliphaz the Temanite, is portrayed as one whose thoughts we should not trust.
22. Isaiah 45:9,10
23. Honore de Blazac, 1799-1850.
24. Samuel Butler, 1835-1902, Notebooks.
25. Wm. Shakespeare, 1564-1616, Hamlet. "A petard is an explosive device for blasting open the doors of fortified structures . ." W Johnson, Record and Services Satisfactory, The Memoir Club, 2003
26. How the Scots Invented the Modern World, A Herman, 2001, Three Rivers Press, NY. p.342
27. J E Morpurgo, Barnes Wallis, Penguin, 1972.
28. Antoine de Saint-Exupery, 1900-44.
29. Samuel Butler, 1835-1902, Erewhon, 1872
30. ibid, Chapter 11
31. Nevil Shute Norway, 1899-1960.
32. George Orwell, 1903-50, in a review of T S Eliot's 'A Choice of Kipling's Verse', in Horizon, Feb. 1942 issue.
33. Luke 10:40-42
34. Rudyard Kipling, 1907. Adopted in the "Ritual of the Calling of an Engineer" in Canada in 1922.
35. 1940-2009, President of Indonesia, 1999-2001
36. The Cambridge Biographical Encyclopedia, David Crystal, Cambridge University Press, 1994, p.C<<1140.
37. St. Teresa of Avila, 1515-82.
38. A Harmon, loc. cit. p.333
39. Linneas (1707-1778). (The author's mentor, W Johnson, FRS, pointed out that quantum physicists would disagree.)
40. Wm. Shakespeare, Henry IV Pt.2. act 3, sc1, I54.
41. Rudyard Kipling, Hymn of the breaking strain, 1935
42. Henry Wadsworth Longfellow, 1807-82.
43. ibid.
44. Progress through Design and Progress through Development, RR Whyte, I Mech, E, London.
45. N L Sadi Carnot, 1796 - 1832
46. Sir Charles A Parsons, 1854 - 1931

47. John Collville, "Footprints in Time" Collins, London 1976.
48. ibid
49. St Matthew,.13:57
50. see "Any colour – so long as it's black", J L Duncan, Exisle Publishing, 2008
51. 1875-1940. Designer of the first high compression petrol engine.
52. Galileo Galilei, 1564 – 1642.
53. The Cambridge Biographical Encyclopedia, D Crystal, CUP, 1994, p.360
54. Confucius, 551-479 BC, Analect 2.15
55. Ralph Waldo Emerson, 1803 – 82, Journal, 1864.
56. Ecclesiastes 3:1-2.
57. Hamlet, act 3
58. Isaiah 30:15,16
59. Webster's New World Dictionary, 3rd Ed.
60. Psalm 104: 14,15, 24–26.
61. Cyril Connolly, 1903-1974, Horizon, Dec.1949-Jan.1950
62. Nikola Tesla, 1856-1943.
63. Margaret Cheney, Tesla: Man Out of Time, Dell Publishing Co. NY, 1981.
64. The 3-phase power system.
65. Montaigne, Book III, Ch.2
66. Wm. Shakespeare, 1564-1616, Twelfth night, act 1.
67. George Orwell, 1903-50, Animal Farm, 1944, Nineteen Eighty-Four, 1949
68. H D Thoreau, 1817-62.
69. Katherine de Pury, 1936-
70. Aristotle, Ethics 1108 al.
71. Confucius, The Analects, 13.21
72. ibid 5.19
73. Eugène Ionesco, The Killer, 1958, "Un functionaire ne plaisante pas."
74. Confucius, Analects 1.16
75. Shakespeare, Julius Caesar, act 3, sc.1
76. Montaigne, vol. II, ch. 1.
77. Montaigne, Bk. III, Ch.9, p.8, quoting Seneca, Ep.,120
78. Seneca, c. 4 BC–65 AD, Letter II, R Campbell et al. The Folio Society, London, 2003.
79. Blaise Pascal, 1623 – 62, Pensées
80. Montagne, Book III, Chap. 1.
81. Book of Common Prayer, Solemnization of Marriage.
82. ibid. XX The Form of the Solemnization of Marriage.
83. Elaine Jordan, Introduction to Jane Austen's Persuasion, Wordsworth Editions Ltd, 2000
84. Jane Austen, 1774-1817, Persuasion, loc.cit.
85. Kahlil Gibran, The Prophet, on Marriage.
86. ibid. on Joy and Sorrow
87. Werner Karl Heisenberg, 1901-1976. uncertainty principal,1927.
88. Arthur Koestler, 1905-83,
89. The Act of Creation,Artur Koestler, London, Hutchinson, 1964
90. Confucius, 551-479 BC, Analect 2.15
91. Charles Dickens, 1812-70, Hard Times, 1852, Mr Gadgrind.
92. Henri Poincaré, 1854-1912.
93. ibid, The Act of Creation
94. ibid
95. ibid, Bk. III, ch. 9.
96. JK Galbraith, American economist, born 1908
97. Montaigne, Bk. 3, ch. 8.
98. Shakespeare, Antony and Cleopatra (1606-7)
99. Psalm 73: 2-6, 16,17
100. Cyril Connolly, 1903-1974, Horizon, Dec.1949-Jan.1950
101. Montaigne, Bk. III, quoting Seneca Ep., 52
102. Martin Buber, 1878-1965
103. Nikolai Alexandrovich Berdyayev, 1874-1948.
104. Proverbs 4:18

ACKNOWLEDGMENTS

Many of the concepts in this book derive from the author's guide, mentor, and friend, RR Whyte, whose brief biography by his son, Robert, is given in the appendix. The author gratefully acknowledges this debt and hopes that he has done full justice to the ideas. The author also thanks those who have commented on earlier drafts of the book, particularly the late Professor W Johnson, FRS, Dr Graeme Heap, and the author's son, John Sanderson Duncan, who happens to be a better writer than his father. The encouragement of family, particularly his wife, Patricia, has been most valuable. During the final stages of preparation, Rachel Starr Thomson's kindly, skilful, and prompt editing has vastly improved the text; she and her team have also taken the whole work through to publication with great care. Thanks also to Robert Whyte, mentioned above, who has contributed much during the final stages of the work.

ABOUT THE AUTHOR

John Duncan was born in Australia in 1932 and graduated in Mechanical Engineering at the University of Melbourne. He served a graduate apprenticeship with Caterpillar Tractor Company in Illinois, USA, and after a number of years in engineering construction in Australia took up an academic appointment at the University of Manchester Institute of Science and Technology. This was followed by academic positions in Canada and New Zealand, and he retired as Professor Emeritus from the University of Auckland in 1998. He was elected as Fellow of the American Society for Metals for his work in education and research in metal forming and is an honorary professor of two universities in China and one in Australia. He has been a member of professional engineering associations in the UK, Canada, and New Zealand and was recently awarded an honorary degree of Doctor of Science by Deakin University, Australia. His principal interest in education has been in engineering design, and he has also published extensively in materials and metal forming.

Professor Duncan and his wife live on a small farm near Auckland with part of their family. They have three children, eight grandchildren, and, at present, one great-grandchild. His hobbies include sailing, boat-building, restoration of historic automobiles, and writing. He has published a book for the general reader on Henry Ford's early design work, *Any Color—So Long As It's Black: Designing the Model T Ford 1906–1908.*

www.ingramcontent.com/pod-product-compliance
Lightning Source LLC
Chambersburg PA
CBHW061728020426

42331CB00006B/1154